THE PAPAS
AND THE
ENGLISHMAN

From Corfu to Zagoria

Roy Hounsell

**Introduced by
John Waller**

YIANNIS BOOKS
England

YIANNIS BOOKS

Acknowledgements

I would like to say that without the enthusiasm and encouragement of Ainley Brownhill (my wife Effie), born and bred in Ilkley, in the West Riding of Yorkshire, it is unlikely any of these events would have happened, and this book would never have reached fruition. And thanks are owed to our good friend Tim Waller and his computer skills for the final editing. And particularly to John Waller, our publisher, who accepted the manuscript for publication.

THE PAPAS AND THE ENGLISHMAN

Published in 2007 by **YIANNIS BOOKS**
101, Strawberry Vale, Twickenham TW1 4SJ, UK

Typeset by Mike Cooper, 25 Orchard Rd, Sutton SM1 2QA
Printed by Antony Rowe, Chippenham, Wiltshire

Front cover: Bridge near Koukouli by Peter Jenkins
Back cover: Koukouli Church by Roy Hounsell
Map of Zagoria by John Chipperfield

224 pp
ISBN 978-0-9547887-3-5

THE PAPAS AND THE ENGLISHMAN

From Corfu to Zagoria

ZAGORIA AND THE VIKOS GORGE

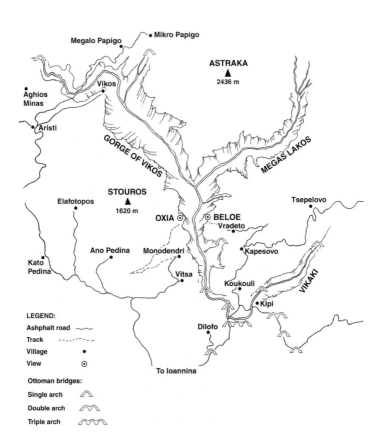

PREFACE

"He's crazed with the spells of Far Arabia.
They have stolen his wits away."

Walter de la Mare

When we first announced our intention of buying a house and living in Zagoria, a virtually unknown area of Greece close to the Albanian border, our friends looked at us askance. Clearly they were thinking, "They're crazed with the spell of far Zagoria. It has stolen their wits away!"

Well, if our wits have been 'stolen away' we can only say we are a good deal happier without them. Our life here, in the village of Koukouli, could not be more contented, more rewarding and trouble free. This is the story of our search for an idyll which, unlike most Holy Grails, we eventually found and held on to. As with all stories it has a beginning and, in our case, that beginning happens to be in Corfu. So, read on – come with us on our quest and delight with us, witless as we are, in that quest's end.

AUTHOR'S NOTES

Some purists will insist that the area of Greece about which I write should more correctly be referred to as Zagori. However, many people are happy to call it Zagoria, a name more rounded, more evocative of distant lands. I invoke artistic licence.

All characters in this book and the places described are real. The observations recorded are mine, and mine alone.

INTRODUCTION

Robert Carver, in the prelude to his book 'The Accursed Mountains' tells how he was interviewing Patrick Leigh Fermor for BBC Radio 3 and, off microphone, asked him "If you were eighteen now, in 1991, and you wanted to go somewhere – somewhere right off the map, with no tourists or modern developments – where would you go?"

He frowned and thought hard for several moments. "Epirus – the north, the mountains. You might have a chance of finding places there."

It was in 1991 that Roy and Effie Hounsell moved into their place in Zagoria.

In 1966, Patrick Leigh Fermor wrote in 'Roumeli – Travels in Northern Greece': "Through the sierras of the Zagora, beyond Vitza and Mondendri where they grazed their flocks in summer, runs the narrow and terrible gorge of Vichou, falling sheer in a chasm to great depth: a dark chaos of boulders and spikes through which, when it is in spate, a tributary of the Aoös river foams with a noise like faraway thunder. But whenever their talk veered to the summer pastures of the Zagora, all their eyes lit up like those of the children of Israel as they thought of Canaan."

It was in 1966 that we fell in love with Corfu. Soon afterwards we built a small summer-house above the deserted west coast.

In spring, as we went over the mountain behind us,

we would look east across olive groves covered in flowers to the twin forts of the town, the silver sliver of sea and the snow-topped mountains of the mainland. In summer, the breeze would cool us under the shade of our huge olive tree and in the evening we would swim off empty beaches. In autumn, after great storms turned the bay far below white as rollers roared in across the open Mediterranean, glorious sunsets towards Italy would herald crystal clear days with the mainland mountains now covered in snow.

Though our trips to the mainland were few, we always visited the majestic monasteries of Meteora but never explored the wild north-west of Greece with its Vikos Gorge and the 46 villages of Zagorochoria. Last October Nick the Pool persuaded us to go and stay with his friend and ex-pool man Roy Hounsell who had left Corfu and turned a derelict house in one of the villages into a bed-and-breakfast.

Less than an hour and a half after leaving Igoumenitsa we crossed the Gorge, near its source, beside a glorious Ottoman style pack-horse bridge and arrived in front of Koukouli church behind which was the square in the village centre – the *plateia* or *mesochori* – with its ancient plane tree in the middle and the exquisite fountain complex to one side. A narrow cobbled path led past houses, some derelict and some restored, to a stone roofed gate and into a tranquil, secluded, sun-trapping courtyard between two rebuilt traditional houses – Roy and Effie's Place.

Two days of self-indulgent tourism followed: beyond Monodendri at the viewpoint of Oxias we had our first sight of the Vikos gorge, the deepest in the world – the Grand Canyon is just a canyon – dropping 1,000 metres into the chasm below; over the top of the pass to the north, we investigated the monument to the Greek Army and the local people who stopped the Italian invasion of the country in

November 1940; at the village of Aristi we stopped for spoonfuls of *Glika*, fruits preserved in sugar and their juices, and a glass of water; we forked right to Vikos with its arcaded church in the *plateia* and another dramatic view of the Gorge; after our return to Aristi we forked left over the Voidamatis river and took a dip in a cool pool before zigzagging up 19 hairpin bends to finish at Megalo then Mikro Papigo and the spectacular view of the *Pyrgi* or 'towers', as they turned pink in the sunset. In the churches we found frescoes and in the mansions magnificent wall paintings. We ate well, first in the little taverna on the Koukouli *plateia* and then at a taverna past the gorgeous three-arched bridge below Kipi. I even heard the haunting Epiriot Clarinet.

Over lazy breakfasts Roy told us of his life in undiscovered Zagoria and the trials and tribulations of re-building the two houses. I found that his story, though twenty years later, mirrored ours in Corfu. Before we left, I mentioned my two books, *Greek Walls* and *Corfu Sunset*.

Out of the blue, he produced his own manuscript. From its pages I found that Roy was quite a character – even if slightly curmudgeonly. He wrote with wicked humour and much feeling. He had restored a little bit of lost Greece in Koukouli and had brought income into a once-dying village. He was no fair-weather lover of Zagoria: in the winter he didn't leave for Athens or abroad but stayed with the remaining fifteen villagers to brave out the snow and the cold. He and Effie have now become part of the village. This is a story that too few of the new migrants to the Mediterranean can tell.

JOHN WALLER
Agios Gordis, CORFU
August 2006

Oh *not* to be in England... !

Corfu in September is a truly beautiful island. The main mob of tourists has beaten a retreat and migrated back to the gloom and wet of the north. The Italians, who spill off large ferry boats onto the island during August, have packed up and gone with their cars, boats, blow-up beach toys and their grandmothers. All the heat and clamour and nerve frazzling intensity of the main tourist season have abated. Magnolia and Jacaranda trees hang heavy with blossom, grapes are ripening on the vines, people are altogether more relaxed and a delightful languor has taken over.

Redundancy, the great leveller, had been instrumental in bringing us to the Greek island of Corfu. The world of Marketing and Advertising is always the first to fall in a recession along with notable trades such as Car Sales and Household Furnishings. With magnificent miscalculation on my part I had moved, after fourteen years of service, from one company to another only to find myself, two years later, made redundant as the Marketing and Advertising Manager of the Household and Furnishing Department.

Thirty eight would not normally appear to be a great age, but in the advertising business it's the same as turning the pages of history backwards. I wrote a convincing C.V. showing a steady track record; went to interviews full of confidence and came back with none. Weeks of this demoralising procedure followed until, in my last interview, the truth was finally driven home to me. The interviewer was a smart young man of about twenty three, well groomed, clean and impeccably dressed in the way all young Account Executives are. He was perfectly polite but kept glancing at his watch as if he had something better he'd rather be doing. Nevertheless we plodded on with the interview until suddenly he started to pack up his papers exactly as though he had come to the end of reading The Nine O'clock News. Looking up, he smiled.

"Without being personal, Mr. Hounsell, I'm afraid that in this day and age you are... how can I put it? Well... just a bit too old for this sort of thing."

I came home with the finality of this news hanging over me to the comfort of my wife, and after supper over a couple of whiskies, we sat by the fire and pondered our future. This recession was not going to disappear overnight. My trade was on its knees and I was over the hill. What possibilities lay ahead for us?

We were late going to bed that night having laboriously poured over various alternatives all of which drew a blank. The one thing we were agreed upon was that we should leave it in our minds for a few days - mull it over while washing up, gardening, cleaning the car, doing the chores. Surely between us we'd come up with something? It took a little longer than we expected but the germ of an idea began to develop.

Many years ago, when I was in my early twenties, way before I met and married Effie, I had spent two wonderful summers working in Greece and loved every minute of it. Probably for all the wrong reasons - sun, sea and girls. However, I had met and got to know quite a number of people during that period. Naturally, over the years, some had drifted away but others had kept in touch. Quite recently we had heard from Valerie and Dionysios, or Dennis as he preferred to be called, telling us they had bought an old olive press on Corfu which they were gradually converting into holiday cottages. The idea we eventually came up with was, quite simply, to phone them and ask whether they thought there could be any possibilities for us out there. Three weeks later we were jet-bound for Corfu.

An early Autumn shower met us at the airport, outsize drops sizzling onto hot tarmac, smelling of scorched pond-water. After the usual formalities as arrivals, not to mention waiting an age for the broken down carousel to resurrect itself, we bundled ourselves and our luggage into a taxi and drove north to 'Casa Lucia', the embryonic empire of Valerie and Dennis.

We had a wonderful reunion. It was evening, and sitting under the great walnut tree at the restaurant they ran, just down the road from their cottage complex, we talked, drank and ate lazily, for hours. All those special flavours, smells and sounds which are Greece once more enveloped us. The sharpness of fresh cut salad dressed with lemon juice and an all pervading scent of oregano; the tang of tzatziki and the mellowing effect of retsina; bunches of gaily coloured geraniums on the tables, candlelight and soft playing bouzoukia; the last late cicadas chirruping and the slender black silhouettes of cypress trees against a darkening sky. After our drinks and food in that warm scented September night we felt totally relaxed.

The following morning, waking up, we forgot for a moment where we were, until the croaking of a tree frog in the passion flower round our cottage window reminded us.

We rendezvoused as arranged at the main house, the original old olive press, which had been restored and converted into Valerie and Dennis's own home. The huge millstones, stone troughs and great wooden screw that operated presses from the old days were no longer in existence. But they had managed to preserve and incorporate two wonderfully curved stone archways that alone supported the great sweep of roof.

Outside on the terrace, under its eaves, breakfasting on yoghurt and honey, we watched with fascination the antics of a family of swallows who had built their mud-packed nest, an upside down igloo, against a protruding beam. From their frantic to-ings and fro-ings, the amount of twitterings and clickings one to another, we worked out that the family were busily getting ready for their long winter vacation. The parents seemed to have several rather stroppy teenagers whom they were trying to organise.

The packing to be done, flight times arranged, milk cancelled, gas and electricity turned off and the house left as they hoped to find it later; frayed nerves, sense of humour failure and family recriminations - you could see it all.

After breakfast Dennis insisted we go with him on a tour of inspection to see everything that had been done so far and what their plans were for the future. Dennis is tall for a Greek, with a handsome lived-in face and broad toothsome smile. Then, just into his fifties, his thick wavy hair was showing a thread or two of matinée idol grey. He'd been brought up in Piraeus, the shipping centre of Greece, once outside and now a part of Athens, where he had trained and become an interior designer of cruise liners. In his work he had travelled the world, seeing and learning a great deal, acquiring standards of perfection that he applied to everything he did but which many of his less exacting compatriots found hard to understand.

"Why go to all that trouble, Dennis?" they would be heard to say, watching him at work. "Why not just do it the ordinary way? No-one will notice the difference."

But the ordinary way was not Dennis's way and it was apparent in all he had built. The attention given to space, to light, the placement of windows, the detail of fittings and the careful planting of trees, creepers, hedges and lawns; we noticed and appreciated everything. With justifiable pride he showed us all his handiwork and described the plans he had for more cottages and a swimming pool with vine covered pergolas for shade. It was all so beautiful and, after recent experiences in England, so exciting and invigorating. Our idea of coming here, of living on Corfu, became more and more attractive. The big question was... what would we do? A holiday island is all very well for a holiday. But permanent holidaying for Effie and me would drive us mad. The novelty of sitting on endless beaches, eating at endless tavernas, drinking endless glasses of cheap wine was not the answer for us. It had no direction and we would soon tire of it. Something had to be found with which we could occupy ourselves, but what? Certainly a one week visit was not going to be long enough to find out.

The solution presented itself, unexpectedly, a couple of evenings later as we sat once more under the walnut tree. Halfway through dinner, as Dennis was pouring us another generous beakerful of retsina, he casually asked: "What would you say to coming out next Spring and helping me finish the cottages?"

Our mouths dropped. This was... perfect! We could help Dennis and Val, find out more about the island and at the same time see if we could find a niche for ourselves. The rest of the evening was spent happily sorting out a multitude of details, and it was agreed and drunk to several times as far as I can remember that we would come out in March or April and work in return for food and accommodation. Excited and slightly wobbly we said goodnight and stumbled into bed to sleep the sleep of the dead.

One more day before the flight back. We hadn't been to a beach during the entire week so we borrowed a scooter and with a 'Treasure Island' kind of tourist map eventually managed to find a perfectly beautiful cove with just three, small tavernas right down on the sea's edge. We'd had to park the scooter some way off as it was only possible to reach the cove by boat or, as we did, by following a goat path along the coast.

"Go to the middle taverna," they'd told us. "It's the best."

And they were right. The food was wonderful and Toula and Thanasis the owners became instant friends. The sea lapped the table legs, little blue and green hand painted fishing boats bobbed quietly against a crazily tilting wooden jetty, and the shores of Albania, within touching distance it seemed, hemmed the horizon. This had to be heaven.

And it was here, whilst in heaven, the momentous decision was made to come out to Corfu; to sell our house in England and buy, instead, a smaller cottage. We lived in Surrey in a two bedroomed, converted Edwardian summer house, set in five acres of land. Prices there are relatively high so it made sense to buy a cottage somewhere where prices were lower, say Cornwall. It would be our funk hole in case things on Corfu failed to work out and we were obliged to return. A couple of celebratory Metaxas sealed the decision.

We did wonder though whether the euphoria of our trip would fade once back in England and faced with the reality of selling our home. Certainly it would be a wrench for we loved it dearly. Would the decisions reached on Corfu vaporise as we settled in again? It turned out not to be the case. Both of us knew that this was something we really wanted to do and we were resolute. Friends, however, appeared less enthusiastic. Some were openly dissuasive and all seemed vaguely suspicious of the whole thing.

Despite their negative attitude we spent the best part of the next three months in and out of estate agents and finally, with more luck than judgement, we succeeded in selling our house and bought a terraced tin miner's cottage in Gunnislake just on the Cornwall side of the Tamar River. Furniture that wouldn't fit in went into storage and, after two weeks of playing house and sorting out paperwork, we were ready to set out for Holland to pick up our new car and from there drive on down to Greece.

Outside Schipol airport there is a huge emporium selling everything imaginable, Duty Free. We had ordered our car, a small 800cc Suzuki jeep, over the phone from England, the size of the engine being dictated by the tax laws on imported cars prevailing in Greece at the time. The car showroom was vast, all sheet glass, highly polished floors, potted plants and motors of every type elegantly displayed. There was a smell of newly sprayed cars eager to be let out of their glass cage, freed to join the world's traffic jams.

We headed off to the sumptuous sales offices where, to our surprise, everything was ready and waiting and, after signing a few papers, we followed 'our man' through the jungle of palms until, suddenly, in a small clearing, there was our silver Suzuki. She looked minuscule! We introduced ourselves and I could swear she purred with excitement. On the front seat was a map of Europe, and on the passenger seat a large bouquet of flowers. Now this was salesmanship indeed. We loaded our bags in the back, the glass doors sighed open and, to the envy of all the rest, one inmate was released.

Shortly afterwards we stopped to consult the map. We were obliged to run our 'Suzi' in and decided to give the motorways a miss. We had time on our hands. There were no deadlines. This was what all the past months had been about. For the next five days we pottered gently south through Belgium, France and Italy, savouring the scenery and cuisine alike, en route. Brindisi is a port at the south eastern tip of Italy, the launching pad for ferry boats bound for Greece and beyond, and a place of most unprepossessing muddle. We managed to find our boat, the Italian run 'Expresso Greco', otherwise known as the 'Expresso Cappuccino' on account of its overall brown and cream livery. The very same boat that I'd travelled to Greece on nearly twenty years earlier. The swimming pool on the upper deck had given way to more profitable parking space and gone were all the in-house television sets which had been the envy of Greek passengers, Greece being without a television service in those bygone days. And, the minute we boarded, tired and hungry from a long day driving, the restaurant promptly closed its doors. We hadn't even raised anchor!

I went to see the Bursar and gave him to understand

that this was ridiculous. What sort of service did they call it when the restaurant was closed to passengers before we'd even left port?

He shrugged his shoulders, pulled down the corners of his mouth, turned and walked away.

Tired, hungry and by now angry into the bargain, I went above to find the Captain. One of the crew tried to bar my way. "You can't go up there," he shouted.

"Just try and stop me, sunshine!"

I found the Captain on the Bridge. He had obviously not long got up from a few hours kip and was busy adjusting his dress in the lower regions.

"Do you speak any English?" I asked.

"A leetle."

"Then can you tell me why they've shut the bloody restaurant?"

"I am thee Capitan, not thee Chef. Go and see thee Bursar."

"I have just seen 'thee Bursar', and he is not in the least bit interested."

The Captain still seemed to be half asleep. Wearily he leaned over and picked up a phone. Words were exchanged. Then... *violent* words. The phone was tucked under his chin and massive, windmill arm movements followed, with heavy poundings of the table in front of him. Then... silence. Gently he put the phone down.

"I 'av reserve a table for you in thee restaurant but please not to tell other passengers."

It was on the tip of my tongue to ask him why not, but I thought better of it. He was the Captain, it was his ship, and I was starving. A bit sheepishly we made our way back to the restaurant. There we received Gold Card service - an excellent meal, superb attention and a delicious wine recommended by the chef. Finishing with coffees and Strega, feeling delightfully replete, we called for the bill. Our waiter... actually, I should say *the* waiter as we were the only people eating in the restaurant, the doors having been firmly locked again on our arrival and all other passengers re-routed to the bedlam of the snack bar. The waiter made a phone call before returning to the table with a folded piece of paper on a saucer. I opened it. It was blank.

"What's this?"

"It ees from ze Capitano. You ees his friends."

Early next morning the boat was cruising slowly down the channel that separates Corfu from Albania, no more than a mile across at its narrowest point. It was here, in 1946, well after peace was declared, that two British warships were blown up by Albanian mines with horrific loss of life. As a consequence, the British impounded Albanian gold reserves deposited with them for safety during the war. Only recently was the gold returned, when the Communist government of Hoxha was ousted. Now, ahead of us to the right, Corfu town emerged through sunlit morning haze, the characteristic shape of the old fortress jutting out to sea, and the charmingly quaint esplanade of old Venetian buildings glowing warm and peach coloured. The Venetians had control of Corfu for over four hundred years from the end of the 14th century and this old part of the town was built by them in the style of their beloved Venice. Slightly faded, crowded together with all its little alleyways, churches, and helter-skelter of roof levels, it is steeped in history and has an air of faded prosperity.

Not so the customs houses. The harbour is just

outside the town and we berthed with the usual clanks and mechanical grindings of dropped anchors and lowered gangplanks. Across a potholed, concrete jetty we were directed to a clump of great rectangular utility sheds with metal framework, prison railings, litter all around and a few struggling eucalyptus trees whose misfortune it was to have been planted there at all. Suzi, of course, had Dutch number plates, and it was here we got our first taste of the logic of Greek bureaucracy. We, as foreigners, were entitled to stay in Greece for three months; the car was entitled to stay for four! Our passports were stamped and Suzi's particulars, including her engine number, which naturally we didn't know and which proved extremely difficult to find, were painstakingly written in the back. Thankfully through and free to go, we set off up the road to Casa Lucia.

Dennis had made progress since last we'd been there and was now hard at work on the Green Cottage; the Blue, Red, and Yellow having all been completed. He and Val had heard of a house nearby which was for rent, and had arranged for us to have an interview with the owners. So, a couple of days later, we went to meet our prospective landlords, half a mile up the road behind Casa Lucia and left up a track through overgrown olive groves. Down a small hill we found a huddle of old buildings, three identical clapped out Fiats in assorted colours and heaps of junk and clutter. Four red setters came lolloping out of nowhere barking and scattering a grey cloud of cats in all directions. At the front door of a rickety porch, rusty guttering dangling overhead, stood our landlord, a silver-haired, roly-poly man in his mid-sixties, with a fine featured face and eyes of angelic blue.

"Welcome," he said softly in English, and led us into the living room.

The house, we discovered, had been built originally as an entertainment villa for summer house-guests, many years ago. It was eight sided, the living room being the centre, with all the other rooms and the porch leading off like a giant honeycomb. Certainly it had seen better days, but when the main house, now a mound of tangled ivy, brambles and moss, had been gutted by fire, they had been forced to make it their home.

Andrée, his wife, was introduced to us, a petite, rather tired looking lady who smoked countless non-tipped cigarettes neatly nipped in half, which she kept in a tin together with a short holder. It was, she said, her way of cutting down but, watching the rate at which the holder was constantly re-loaded, I failed to follow her theory. Over drinks we learnt that her family had been one of the largest aristocratic families in Greece. As a young girl she had lived like a princess and been educated by a series of foreign nannies as a consequence of which she was fluent in five languages, including English. I still have a copy of an old map of Corfu where this whole extensive tract of countryside, which was Andrée's inheritance, bears the family name. But, times had changed and death duties taken their toll.

Andrée suggested that we go with Spyros, her husband, to look at the house they had for rent so we followed him, chugging in one of the veteran Fiats, back the way we had come. Halfway up the track he jerkily took a right hand turn. After another three hundred yards through olive trees, rounding a sudden tight bend, the house stood above us against the skyline.

It had been built, Spyros said, by the Venetians as a store for ammunition, a small garrison to protect surrounding houses against marauding pirates or, worse,

Turks. 'Paleomagaza' was its name, meaning 'old store' or 'magazine' in this case. So dilapidated did it appear to us that day, its history was hard to credit. We fought through weeds to the front door and when finally that was forced open, a terrific smell of damp and mildew engulfed us. The house had not been lived in for over five years and it was apparent everywhere.

However, there were two bedrooms, a good bathroom, decent kitchen and an impressive cavern of a living room with a darkly beamed and raftered ceiling. An arched window to the right gave onto a sheer drop with fantastic views over the tops of olive trees interspersed with pencil slim cypresses leading down to the sea, and beyond to the snow clad mountains of Northern Greece and Albania. We were led through heavy studded doors on the opposite side of the room into the so-called garden.

It was littered with old piping, tin cans, buckled old buckets, bed frames, sheet iron and piles of gravel and broken bricks! This man Spyros had a positive mania for junk. Peering through the waving asphodels it was possible with enormous imagination to envisage a garden. Paleomagaza - and already the name had acquired a hold on us - stood on its own hill with an acre of land that was completely flat and walled all around with mossy grey stones. Andrée and Spyros' house and this stood in splendid isolation on four hundred acres. We squinted into the sun, and the rubbish and debris disappeared. Yes, it could all be made to look lovely, but it was going to be hard work.

We moved in shortly afterwards and set to with brooms, mops, paint, bleach and plenty of hot water. The house started to take shape. I had brought out some tools from England and across the garden was a mouldering stone building, with a reasonably sound roof, which soon became my workshop. We hacked back asphodels and weeds, and got rid of all the old junk, revealing flower beds with bushes of shoulder-high geraniums. We bought pots, scrounged plants, pruned back, and after a few months it really began to feel like home. Added to this we acquired a cat called 'Batty' who, we were assured, was essential for keeping down the snakes and tree rats which apparently infested the roof.

Meanwhile we were helping Dennis finish the Green cottage in time to meet the deadline Val had set by taking a booking for it in August. The day before the guests were due to arrive he and I were crawling on all fours putting a third coat of varnish on the skirting boards. The cottage was actually finished and ready, this was typically an extra 'Dennis Detail'. On our knees with our pots of varnish we suddenly became aware that someone was standing in the doorway. Without a word we turned as one, brushes poised.

"Good afternoon. Is this the Green cottage?"

"Yes," we replied in unison.

"I'm awfully sorry. My name's Pearson and my wife and I have arrived a day early, I do hope it's not too inconvenient."

"Not at all," replied Dennis affably as he got up, to be faced with the problem of what to do with his paintbrush before he could shake hands.

I don't know what happened to that first summer, it went by so fast. A new environment perhaps, new things to do, exploring the island, meeting people - whatever, it had gone. And still we had not found the niche that would earn us some money. We'd have to find something fairly soon because in October, when our summer working arrangement at Casa Lucia came to an end, we would be taking on the rent for Paleomagaza.

The Gallery Inn was our local in Corfu Town, run by an English woman and her Dutch husband, 'Reuters', for English speaking residents and a hot-bed of gossip. One lunchtime, we overheard a conversation there about a 'Jim' who ran his own small business installing and equipping swimming pools. He was having to quit and leave Corfu because his wife was unable to cope with the heat and had become homesick for England. I paid passing attention because I knew absolutely nothing about swimming pools. Then the very next day, to our surprise, Jim made contact with us. His big problem was that, although due to leave within the week, he hadn't found anybody to take over the servicing of his pools and was desperate not to let his clients down. Would we be interested in taking them on?

We weren't at all sure, but agreed to accompany him next day to visit his pools and meet the owners. And it struck us that, having nothing else in the offing, we might just as well give this a try. With the owners away for most of the year there was the possibility for potential spin off if we could obtain the annual maintenance and management of their villas and gardens as well, something Jim had not been interested in doing. In the short time available before Jim left, diagrams were drawn up of all the various pumphouses, and meticulous notes made as to which valve did what. We were fed a crash course on chlorine levels and PH balance, introduced to pool equipment suppliers, engineers, pump specialists, electricians, until our heads were reeling, and finally landed with Jim's end-of-line stocks of chemicals.

Then he was gone, and we found ourselves alone with six pools to service! I realize now that a swimming pool, properly built and with modern equipment, is not such a devastatingly difficult thing to manage but in those early days we made some awful mistakes. Fortunately for us it was at the end of the season and we had no irate clients to witness our first incompetent fumblings. I remember one pool in particular. For some reason, most probably in that final rush, Jim had not given us the proper sequence for the valves for backwashing the filter. A sparkling clear pool turned a murky green before our very eyes. We were appalled! What had we done? Falling into the pumphouse to switch everything off, we checked and rechecked our notes. We'd followed Jim's instructions to the T. Laboriously we talked our way, stage by stage, through the system, ignoring the notes, until suddenly it dawned. By wrongly turning a valve we had successfully blasted all the sand out of the filter into the pool! School art lessons confirmed that blue (pool water) plus yellow (sand) make green.

So, what to do? Ignorance combined with cunning. We left the sand to sink to the bottom for two days and then sucked it up with the pool vacuum straight back into the filter.

It took time but with practice we got the hang of it all and learned, as well, that every pool has its own little ways of playing up and making a fool of you. Since we had persuaded most of our pool owners that it would be a good idea for us to take care of their houses and gardens as well, we enjoyed our first winter on Corfu happily employed and well content with our new life.

Winter passed into Spring - and Easter. Easter is the most important of the Greek Religious festivals and Corfu, in particular, is renowned for the splendour of its celebrations. People from all over flock to the Island to join in, and that included our clients. It's a hectic time for everybody preparing for the event and has something of the feeling of getting a stage set up in time for the opening night. It was too cold to swim but we had our pools sparkling, the houses were immaculate and everyone well pleased. As our first trial it was a success and a great relief to us both.

The following summer was spent working and seeking out new houses and pools to add to our growing list. We had not realised just how much the heat and humidity would affect us, combined with daily battling on the roads against armies of heedless tourists. By the end of the season, though pleased with what we had achieved, we felt utterly exhausted and in need of a break. A friend suggested going over to the Greek mainland to a mountainous region known as Zagoria, an area at the very north of Epirus bordering Albania. It was, they said, wild, almost deserted and very spectacular. The idea appealed and so, the very next week we took ourselves off.

The drive through Epirus from Igoumenitsa, the mainland port where we landed by ferryboat, was utterly different from our recent experiences on Corfu. Near empty roads, dense mature woodlands, great rushing rivers, lush well cared for farmland, low humidity and, once away from the coast, not an olive tree in sight. It was another world. We went slowly, following our map, soaking it all in until, with a sweeping left hand bend out of an upland plateau, we found ourselves in Zagoria.

This whole area has been designated a National Park and includes forty-six villages all protected against modern architectural abominations. Everything, we discovered, was built of stone: stone walls, stone houses, and stone roofs.

Even the streets, for the most part too narrow to drive down being no more than the width of a donkey with panniers, were intricately cobbled with stones. Each house, or mansion for some were very large, had high walls all around with a stone lychgate and solid wooden doors opening into a perfectly private, paved courtyard. None of the villages straggled, each clung to the hillside in tight formation, blending absolutely with the landscape.

Monodendri was, we understood, one village where it was possible to find rooms for the night. Arriving at the outskirts of the village we parked the car and walked on into the village square. A massive plane tree stood in the centre spreading its huge arms over the entire 'plateia'. A rather smart looking taverna alongside, built in sparkling white stone with high arched windows, looked inviting and seemed a good starting point for enquiring about a room. Inside we found a good log fire burning, and a delightful elderly couple running the establishment. We ordered some wine whilst they sent off a young lad in search, they said, for Mister (Kyrios) Menelaus. Sometime later he returned with Menelaus in tow, a small sprightly man, his dark donkey jacket worn jauntily across his shoulders over a baggily large brown striped suit. His hair was astonishingly white and thick round a spare, well chiselled face with twinkling, bird-bright eyes. He introduced himself and said he had a 'room traditional'. Curious, we followed him down and along cobbled streets to 'Spiti Menelaus', 'House of Menelaus'.

The room, it turned out, certainly was traditional, steeped in historical, Turkish influenced features: a graceful, bowed fireplace with deep hearthstone and low beds, or banquettes, on either side; wall paintings, carved wooden niches; an ornate wooden ceiling with the incongruous addition of a dangling electric wire ending in a naked lightbulb; and heavy bedcoverings of local weave. It was wonderful - we would take it. Menelaus proudly showed us the bathroom. By contrast this was surprisingly modern with bidet, bath, toilet and handbasin all in matching fawn with gleaming chrome taps.

Having strolled around the village for an hour, getting chilled we returned to the taverna. It was seven o'clock and we asked, like a couple of idiot tourists, for the menu.

"We don't have a menu. We only serve cheese pie."

Obviously we should have known this.

"Oh, fine. Well, in that case... um, yes, we'll have the cheese pie."

Apart from greatly speeding up the process, this method of ordering certainly saves a lot of arguing and indecision. Half an hour later, the elderly little lady came staggering out of the kitchen with a giant plate, the size of a dustbin lid, piled high with crocodile-bite chunks of cheese pie. This couldn't possibly be just for us - it must be for everybody in the restaurant. But no, tottering between the tables she landed it fair and square on ours. I could hardly see Effie over the top. Bracing ourselves we set to and found it was delicious. Thin crispy squares of cheese crumbled into a light batter and baked in olive oil. Washing it down with the light, slightly pétillant Zitsa wine, the pile reduced but we were definitely struggling. Rescue came in the form of Menelaus who, ordering another bottle of wine, sat himself down and without more ado helped himself to the remainder.

At about eleven, tiredness helped by wine and the open fire drove us out into a bitter night. We headed, teeth chattering, for our 'room traditional'.

To our surprise we found a small, round wood-burning stove pumping out heat, bang in the middle of the room, the stovepipe running up and across and out through a window pane.

"That wasn't there before," said Effie.

"Are you sure?"

"Positive".

"Well... it's a touch you wouldn't get in the Hilton."

A knock at the door produced a beaming Menelaus, a heap of logs in his arms, enough to see us through to morning. Upon entering the bathroom, though, in all its modern magnificence, we discovered jugs and bowls of icy cold water everywhere. Research showed that, apart from waste pipes, nothing was actually plumbed. We mentioned this small point at breakfast and with a wry smile Menelaus told us that he was planning ahead for when mains water would be connected to the village. They had got as far as Vitsa, the village lower down, he said, and they should be up to Monodendri in two, maybe three years.

We used Spiti Menelaus as our base for exploring other parts of Zagoria. Monodendri is conveniently central and has the added attraction of being situated on the edge of one end of the Vikos Gorge, the largest gorge in Europe being eleven miles long and three and a half thousand feet at its deepest. Just outside the village is an ancient monastery overlooking this ravine, clinging to the side of towering cliffs defying gravity. Awestruck and vertigo-satisfied, we set off in Suzi gently touring as I imagine one would have done in the Twenties in England. Slowly, with hardly any traffic just the odd flock of sheep or goats holding us up, allowing time to take in and absorb the never-ending glories of the landscape.

We stopped at other villages and marvelled at the

huge houses, schools and churches. The question baffling us was, obviously there must have been considerable wealth at the time these villages were built, but where could it have come from? This was not farming terrain. All we saw were a few village plots, carefully tilled and tended, but no evidence at all of anything that could have produced such prosperity. In the village squares we sat under the plane trees sipping chipero, a locally brewed hooch not unlike grappa, ideally suited to mountain air. The food served was simple home-made fare, mainly pies like the one in Monodendri with fresh baked bread, local vegetables and cheeses. Time ran on unhindered, and then ran out. Our fifth day, and we were back on the road to dismal Igoumenitsa and the ferry.

It had been a wonderful break, but... back to work. It was easier now that the summer heat had evaporated and our batteries were recharged. But there was something that kept nagging at us, and I realised this was brought on every time we looked out of our living room window at the view of those distant mountains. That was where we had been. Our holiday, it seemed, had turned out to be more than just a relaxing time - we had fallen under the spell of Zagoria. The idea of having a weekend cottage in one of the villages came, and as suddenly went. You would need a contact up there for such a plan. We didn't have one and our Greek was not up to the task, so the idea was shelved. Even so, we could never look at those mountains without feeling strangely drawn to them.

A house in Zagoria?

Life on Corfu continued to be fun and after three years we had built up our business to the point where we could manage it and live comfortably without stress. Through the summers the more sceptical of our English friends had come to stay, scrounged a holiday and left, disappointed to find us well and thriving.

In Greece there are fourteen public holidays and many more local Saints' Days. We were sitting in the garden one morning towards the end of February, reading the previous day's newspapers. Warm sun, clear skies and the fact that it was 'Clean Monday' had convinced us that the best thing to do was to stay quietly at home. Clean Monday is the public holiday which falls on the first day of Lent, so called because, after the previous weeks of Carnival and heavy eating, Greek housewives traditionally clean all their pots, pans and cooking utensils in readiness for the preparation of their special Lenten dishes. Families join together and go out into the countryside en masse. The children fly kites; grown ups lounge with a drink and talk; and the long picnic lunch features the 'Lagana', a flat loaf of bread sprinkled with sesame seeds baked only for this one occasion.

Having settled ourselves down to a peaceful day at home it came as a surprise when the door bell jangled. It was a friend of Sue and Pericles, sent down to invite us to join their Clean Monday celebrations. Hopelessly muttering some feeble excuses that were clearly unacceptable we gave in and conceded we would be delighted to.

Sue and Pericles, their daughter and three sons, were one of the Anglo Greek families we had got to know well since coming to the Island. They lived about half an hour's drive away in a modern house built on the edge of an olive grove with spectacular panoramic views. The place was full of adults and children swarming like ants from the kitchen to the verandah. A gaily covered ping-pong table was being loaded with plate after plate of food: specially prepared meatless dishes, tomatoes gleaming in olive oil and sprinkled with basil, stuffed vine leaves, grilled prawns, taramasalata, bowls of olives and mounds of Lagana. With an assortment of chairs, stools, upended pails and plantpots, twenty-five people down to enjoy it.

The afternoon had a long, drawn-out, dreamy quality; people moving slowly about, the children and their fathers struggling to fly kites in the breathless, heavy air and returning to the table defeated; wine jugs being emptied and replenished; plates stacked in dizzy piles disappearing to the kitchen. Guests gradually began to leave and the group narrowed down to a few stragglers who were variously helping clearing away and washing up. And this was the moment when we were introduced to Eleni, an attractive woman with a wonderfully clear, peach-like complexion and intelligent eyes behind lightly tinted glasses. She spoke quietly, with ease, and had an air of calm self-possession. We discovered that she had been Sue and Pericles' architect when they built their house, but her base was on the mainland and she specialised in restoring old houses in Zagoria. Did we know Zagoria?

Our hearts missed a beat. Yes! We know Zagoria!

Once our pulses had settled, we talked about our visit and she told us of her involvement there. Tentatively we asked if she thought it might be possible to find a weekend cottage for us. Eleni had expressed some surprise that we knew of Zagoria at all but was even more taken aback by our request. However, a loose agreement was made that she would let us know of anything that came her way. Talk moved on to other things and the time came for us to take our leave.

After a long silence in the car Effie said, "What do you think?"

"I don't know. She didn't seem over enthusiastic to me."

And we left it at that.

A month later we received a message from Sue and Pericles. Could we go over to Zagoria next weekend? Eleni had a couple of properties that might interest us. And so, come Friday we were on the ferry and back up the same road from Igoumenitsa we had taken three years earlier, but this time with a different purpose. Eleni had asked us to go straight to her house in the village of Ano Pedina, past the turn off to Monodendri, through a wide plain and on up the hillside. Ano Pedina is rather unique in that the road instead of stopping at the edge of the village, or by-passing it above or below, runs directly through the centre, the houses piled up against each other to left and right behind lines of severely-pollarded poplars.

Up, and seemingly ever up, we passed a children's playground, a church with Byzantine turreted apse, the square with its plane tree, the bust of some solemn moustached elder, erect and bird splattered, a communal well, and finally the kafeneon with a jumble of old metal chairs and tables under the leafiness of false acacias. We pulled in to the side of the road and got out. The kafeneon was closed, the village seemingly deserted. There was absolute silence. A solitary chicken suddenly burst squawking out of a doorway, flew-walked across the road and vanished. Again, silence. Just about now we should hear the clinking of spurs, feel the warm breath of a mule, and turn to find a cheroot-chewing Clint Eastwood standing behind us. It felt like being in an empty film set. Since Eleni hadn't told us where her house was, there was nothing to do but sit and wait. A bird flew down, pecked at the gravel and flew away. And then, this almost deafening silence was broken. Could it be a car? Yes, it was, and a minute later a battered Renault Five came staggering up the steep hill with Eleni at the wheel.

Her house was only a short walk from the kafeneon and we entered through the stone lychgate into the courtyard. To the left was an enchanting building, windows painted a lustrous blue, which had been converted into four bedrooms with ensuite bathrooms. She told us we would be sleeping in number 2, up the stone steps and through the door of the little stone roofed balcony. Opposite was a much bigger building where there were going to be another five rooms, a bar restaurant and kitchens. A small, country hotel. For the moment Eleni's mother, Toula, was running things. A brisk little lady of irrepressible energy she never stopped talking from the moment we walked in. Whether one understood or not she burbled on undaunted, with nods and winks, eyes up, eyes down, facial movements of distress, happiness or gloom – a single dramatic performance totally upstaging and subduing everybody else. Over dinner, with innumerable and unavoidable interruptions from Toula, we explained to Eleni that we were basically looking for a cottage, somewhere to escape to when it became unbearably hot and overcrowded on Corfu. She proved entirely sympathetic. Her husband was a lecturer at the university there and longed for the days when he could get away from the heat and bustle, back to the airiness and solace of Zagoria.

The following day Eleni took us to the village of Kipi, set upon a hill around which two rivers converge and flow away, under an impressive three arched bridge, on into the Vikos Gorge. Built in 1814, the bridge spans over two hundred feet of riverbed, its massive central arch soaring forty feet high, a stunning example of early nineteenth-century stonemasonry. The first house we were shown there was a disappointment. It was on a dark corner with no view other than a horrid mishmash of telephone and electrical cables. It had no garden and was completely overlooked by most of the village. I couldn't see us enjoying pleasant weekends there. We moved on to the next property which came as a bit of a surprise. It was being used as the local Police Station. A large mansion, architecturally interesting for having a Palladian doorway with pillars and iron railed balcony overhead and, being in use, well maintained. The owner, it transpired, lived in Australia and had decided to 'get it off his hands'. The idea of dealing with a Greek in Australia was daunting, not to mention the thought of having to evict the local Police! We didn't feel, somehow, that this would be a popular move for two foreigners hoping to make an entrée into the area. The rest of the day was spent looking at piles of stone, broken down buildings with no services or so far away from any access road as to make rebuilding an impossible task.

Meanwhile, back in Ano Pedina, Toula had been busy. In the corner of a small stone outhouse she had lit an open fire under a large trivet. On top of the trivet she had put a pan three feet in diameter filled with chicken, carrots, potatoes, onions, goodness knows what else, and masses of fresh herbs. Above this, suspended from the rafters on a chain, was a large domed lid with steel bands around it in the form of terracing. We were in time to watch her lower the lid onto the cauldron, scoop up hot ash from the fire with a small shovel and pack it around the terraces until it was completely covered. In an instant she had created an oven with even heat above and below.

We sat for the next hour stoking the fire and replenishing the lid until Toula deemed the food cooked. It was indescribably succulent, aromatic, with the vegetables retaining their individual flavour and texture, and the gravy... sheer perfection! So good was it that for the moment even Toula was reduced to silence. While we were absorbed in eating, Eleni mooted the point that in Zagoria it was going to be much easier to find a large house than a small one. Very few people were willing to sell the smaller buildings, preferring to hold onto them as storerooms or a place to keep their animals in winter. And if we bought a larger house, we could always turn part of it into 'rooms', or even a small hotel like hers. This last sentence was spoken with deliberate slowness, to gauge our reaction. Well, it was certainly not something we had thought of, or even intended. But neither was it an idea to be dismissed out of hand.

At breakfast, sensing our disappointment with the previous day, she suggested we go with her to visit some clients in Papingo, to the north of the Vikos Gorge from Monodendri. Before the modern roads were made, the villages were linked by cobbled and stepped mule paths, ascending and descending culverts, taking the shortest possible route. But the road has to wind and weave round mountain masses and zigzag up hills, making the drive to Papingo a good hour. Papingo, and the smaller Mikro Papingo, are two villages at the very end of the line, tucked against the looming foothills of Gamila with the towering cliffs of Astraka and the great cleft of the Vikos Gorge to one side. The scenery is spectacular and, as the sun moves on its diurnal course, the lighting effects almost theatrical. Approached in morning sun, the massive peaks of rock, aptly called the 'Towers of Papingo', thrust into the sky, shadowy, hazy, indefinable, looking for all the world like a mammoth Victorian jellymould. But in the afternoon, every crevasse, every buttress, every shade of rock is revealed, startlingly defined, and they appear frighteningly vast. It seemed strange that people should have chosen to build their villages in such a desperately isolated and inaccessible place. But that, I suppose, was the very reason - inaccessible to marauding bands of Turks and Albanians. Life up here must have been hard indeed for those original inhabitants.

Eleni's clients in Papingo were converting a group of buildings into a sizeable hotel. The first stage, in the main house, was complete. There were six bedrooms in the local style: fireplaces with low beds on either side, wooden ceilings, barred windows, and the bathrooms thoughtfully discreet as modern necessities. A separate building housed a small kitchen with an old bread oven, a sunny breakfast room and terrace. The next stage was to rebuild a tumble of old barns to make living accommodation for themselves, more rooms and a small conference hall. Nikos and Polly Saxonis had previously lived in Athens, got fed up with the rat race and opted for Papingo, planning, through business connections, to host seminars and small conferences at their hotel as well as catering for holidaymakers.

On the way back, passing through the village of Aristi, we stopped at yet another of Eleni's projects. Here, the original house had been beautifully restored, but against it stood a concrete skeleton, the sort of thing we were so accustomed to see in Corfu and which invariably ended up as some featureless monstrosity. However, we were assured that building would continue in stone, the roof would be stone slated and, by the time it was finished, the extension would be indistinguishable from the original. It was hard to imagine, looking at it, but reassuring to think that such care was being taken to preserve the visual charactcristics of these villages. The owner, his wife and three sons were planning to open and run... a small hotel!

Everyone we met had been enthusiastic and hospitable and we were beginning to wonder whether this tour of would-be hotels was Eleni's quiet way of backing up her idea that we should think of buying a bigger house. That evening we agreed that we were prepared to look at any property for sale, either as a house just for us, or as a possible hotel. Not that we were exactly smitten with the idea of becoming hoteliers but, on the other hand, Corfu was progressively defacing its charming and very lovely characteristics and we found ourselves becoming increasingly disenchanted with it. An hotel in Zagoria? It was a thought.

Months later we were summoned again. This time we were looking at a mansion in Ano Pedina, just off the main street.

37

In the courtyard was a small, two storied building; the lower part with an open archway housed the well, and a wooden staircase led up to what would have been servants' quarters. The main house was impressively large even by Zagorian standards. An aged family retainer had come up from Ioannina by taxi with the key. Heavy front doors unlocked, we walked into a large, windowless vault with doors leading off on one side to two other rooms. At the far end was an elegant, curving staircase with sunlight flooding down, which took us up to the summer level. Exactly the same configuration - one vast reception room with two leading off. But the ceiling! I never thought I would fall in love with a ceiling. Wooden, carved in its entirety with scallops, bunches of grapes, birds, flowers; painted and gilded it was a masterpiece of intricate design. It was possible to buy a ceiling like this and get a house along with it? Through Eleni, who by now had become both agent and friend, we made contact with the owners, three middle aged brothers who had inherited the property and were wanting to sell. Price was agreed, papers would be drawn up and we were delighted. We had taken photographs of the house from all angles and spent happy hours drawing up plans. We would live in the wellhouse and attached outbuildings, and the main building would be the hotel with reception, bar, dining rooms, six bedrooms... ideas abounded.

Some days later, Eleni contacted us. There was a problem. The son of one of the brothers had objected to the sale of the house on the grounds that his father and uncles were selling his inheritance. This was a new one on us. Surely inheritance was a matter dealt with after someone had died, not before? They all trooped off to consult the family lawyer where I imagine an all holy row took place because no agreement was reached. The entire affair, therefore, had to be referred to a special Court Tribunal which only convened once every two years! At this point we lost interest and with it, our ceiling.

In retrospect, downcast though we were at the time, it was fortuitous because we came to realise that the house had very little outside space to offer and it faced quite the wrong way to get much sun. Moreover, the episode awoke us to the fact that a large part of Greek law is based on French Napoleonic law, particularly where property is concerned. Greeks seldom make wills and any inheritance is equally divided amongst surviving relatives. It's not unknown for a house to be owned by six or more people, not necessarily still living in Greece. All inheritors must sign the sale documents on the same day in a notary's office in the area, so already problems arise. The Rubik's cube part of the equation is that, should these six family members agree to sell (a near miracle in itself), it is still possible at any time during the next twenty years for a seventh relative to pop up from somewhere and legally claim his portion - a seventh share of the property as it stands at the time, with all the improvements and increase in value. This sounded positively criminal to our English minds, and our lawyer in Corfu told us in block capitals, 'Buy nothing unless it has CLEAN TITLES!' A sound piece of advice which effectively knocked quite a few potential purchases on the head.

Another visit to the mainland produced a further angle on the hazards of house buying in Greece. The house, once an old school, with uninterrupted views across a valley down to the river, was owned by a Greek who had moved to live and work in Stuttgart. He had bought it two years previously and was sole owner, so we knew the titles were 'clean', his intention being to provide a base in

Greece for his children should they feel the call of their homeland and wish to return. But since the children showed no sign whatever of wanting to leave Germany, even for a short visit, he had decided to sell. His brother who lived in the village showed us around. The house was structurally sound having recently been re-roofed, and had potential. It faced the right way (we carried a compass with us now) and had a sizeable though derelict garden. Questioned about the price, the brother gave us a figure in drachmas the equivalent of £8,000, but said he would need to phone Stuttgart to confirm that. No reply. Not to worry, he would keep trying over the weekend. If we could phone Stuttgart from Corfu on Tuesday evening - he carefully and neatly wrote down the number for us - we would get an answer.

The owner's wife must have been on standby because, when we finally got through, the phone was snatched up after the second ring and she informed us, in strident and heavily accented Greek, that nothing short of £16,000 could possibly be considered for their magnificent property! The trouble is, so many Greeks take it for granted that all foreigners are rolling in money and therefore an easy touch. So, over the weekend the owner of the house (or maybe his wife?) had doubled the price. We didn't even bother to tell them what they could do with their 'magnificent property'.

And so it went on, with visits back and forth, producing nothing but a little more hard won experience. The months rolled by and 'a House in Zagoria' had fallen from the top of our list of aspirations to the very bottom, sadly labelled "No Go". It was at this low point we were yet again summoned by Eleni.

"I think this is it," she said. "How soon can you come over?"

"Give us a few days," we answered.

Lying in bed awake that night I announced to Effie, who was on the point of falling asleep, that we would not be going to the mainland in Suzi.

"Not go in Suzi?" came her astonished reply. "Why ever not?"

"Because we've been hacking back and forth to Zagoria for the best part of four years and the car is well known by now. Even the shepherds on the hills recognise it, and when they all meet up in the village tavernas at night I know darned well what they'll be saying - 'I see those English are still looking for a house'. And BANG! - Up goes the price. No. I'm going to hire a perfectly ordinary, nondescript little car so they won't know it's us!"

Effie muttered something about "complete madness", turned over and fell asleep.

So, in a horrid little red Panda, we made the familiar trip to Zagoria and Ano Pedina and in the afternoon, with Eleni on board, drove the few miles to the village of Koukouli. Parking outside the old church with lovely low arches all along one side, we set off to find the man who was key holder for the owner. This time the owner lived in Igoumenitsa, a bit closer to hand than Australia or Germany. A short way down a walled lane we came upon a neat little house and within moments found ourselves hustled inside and jammed into a small kitchen together with four children and their parents. Mother was a tiny, cuddly woman in her late twenties with short, dark hair, sparkling uptilted eyes and high cheekbones - a merry face, forever beaming.

Her husband, not so much taller, was a wiry, well proportioned man with tangled black hair and beard, an instant Hollywood smile and dark, expressive eyes. He

41

wore unlaced trainers, faded paint-spattered jeans and a yellow tee-shirt with 'Super-Sport' emblazoned across the front. A wooden cocktail stick, stuck behind his right ear, poked out through his hair. The chipero bottle and glasses appeared and, duly fortified, we followed him some sixty yards from his house up another narrow lane to the property.

No traditional gateway greeted us here, but a rather dreadful wrought iron affair from the sixties. Inside was a jungle of prize-winning nettles. There were two, separate, two-storied buildings, the smaller directly to the right of the gate and the larger beyond. Both faced due south. Both were uninhabitable. A large walled garden wrapped right round the houses and at the back, because they were set into the hillside, the roofline was no higher than a man. Certainly there was a lot of work to be done. Walls would have to come down and be rebuilt, new roofs put on, but we were not dismayed. Of all the houses we had looked at there was something about these that had the right 'feel'. They were accessible for building work, they had the advantage of being connected to electricity and mains water, enjoyed total privacy and, what's more, the owner, Mr. Ferandinos, had bought them outright in 1963 - CLEAN TITLES! He was a shepherd and every summer brought his flocks up from Igoumenitsa to graze, taking them back down in the autumn. The houses had been bought as his summer base but because of old age, and a lack of interest amongst his sons for shepherding, he had sold his livestock and was now selling his base. The price was £7,000. Eleni was right. After all our failures we knew, definitely, this was it.

Our friendly keyholder, who spoke no English but had contrived to make himself extremely likable, insisted we stop again at his house for more chipero and 'mezedes', a bite to eat. On our return to the car I said to Eleni:

"He's a nice chap. What does he do?"

"Who, Kostas? Oh, didn't I tell you? He's the Papas. The village priest."

Buying the house – a saga

Mr. Ferandinos, Eleni told us, had previously found a buyer but had lost him when, at the final moment in the notary's office, he had demanded more money. To make certain that he wouldn't play a similar trick on us, it was agreed that in all her dealings with him she would refer to us as 'her clients', never mentioning our names or that we were English. After the Stuttgart experience we had learnt that as foreigners we were target practice for gazumping. The property had to be surveyed and there was no existing 'topographico'. We, not the vendor, had to pay for this to be done. Mr. Ferandinos required a deposit which we paid. Our lawyer in Corfu, Spyros Dalianis, seemed fairly happy with these arrangements, as happy as any lawyer ever is, but insisted on having a paper from the President of Koukouli declaring that Mr. Ferandinos was sole owner of, and in 1963 had legally bought, the property. Spyros explained that as the original purchase was made over twenty years ago this document would give us immunity against the previous owner's relatives, as well as any of Ferandinos', popping out of the woodwork making claims.

The first paper the President produced was not good enough - too many loopholes. So, Spyros drafted out the wording he considered foolproof, and we scuttled off to the Post Office to fax a copy to Eleni in Ioannina who was acting as our go-between. A few days later we got word that she had the new document on her desk signed by the President. To try and speed things up, she was giving it to the driver of the Ioannina/Igoumenitsa bus with instructions to hand it to the Captain of the 6.30 ferry to Corfu! Would I please be on the quayside at 8.30 when the ferry was due to dock, and pick it up.

It was a cold, wet February night. The port was deserted and the streetlights cast shimmering reflections across the wet tarmac. A couple of gaunt dogs prowled, stiff legged round the puddles. I stood against the sidewall of the Port Police Kiosk to shelter from the rain. Two uniformed men inside its brilliantly lit interior sat chain smoking, playing cards, So reminiscent was it of an old black and white movie that, standing in the shadows with my collar turned up and my hands thrust deep in my pockets, I felt like the spy. The lights of the ferry hove into sight, it moored and the ramp clunked down. Two cars trickled off and drove away. The crew worked in silence with ropes and levers and then a solitary figure, head down into the wind, came off the boat. We walked towards each other and met. I told him my name and asked if he had something for me from Eleni Pangratiou. Unzipping the front of his leather bomber jacket, he withdrew a buff envelope and passed it to me. I thanked him, palmed him a thousand drachma note, we shook hands and walked away in opposite directions. I couldn't rid myself of the feeling that I had somehow been involved in some criminal act, and was heartily glad to climb into Suzi and drive home to a warm fire and friendly surroundings.

Years ago Effie and I had formed a fully fledged Greek Limited Company, and we were buying the house through the Company. It was necessary to increase the capital of the Company to enable the purchase to go ahead.

A fairly straightforward procedure involving our lawyer and accountant and, we were to discover, time. Spyros Dalianis instructed us to get from the accountant a declaration that all taxes had been paid over the years and to have the declaration verified by the tax office. An appointment was made with the accountant. He didn't turn up but his gofer did, only to inform us that Lakis had been called away to a funeral in Ioannina. The weekend passed and we elected to be at his office by 8.30 on the Monday morning. At 9.30 the gofer turned up. The weather on the mainland was very bad and the ferries weren't running, so Lakis was stuck in Igoumenitsa. Better try again later in the day. So, back we went in the evening. This time Lakis was home but wasn't coming into the office until the next morning. When finally we collared him, he announced that what we were asking him to do was a lawyer's job, not an accountant's! At this point we both experienced a total sense of humour failure and rushed over to Spyros' office to report Lakis' unhelpful attitude.

Spyros hit the roof, and we had to stand by in embarrassment while he berated Lakis over the telephone, telling him in no uncertain terms what he thought of him, demanding he produce the papers. All very well except that now we found ourselves caught in the middle of a war of professional jealousies. They refused to speak to each other any more over the phone, and we spent an entire week camping outside their respective offices trying to catch them, pleading with them to come to some kind of joint agreement and produce the necessary document. After a highly tense meeting in Spyros' office, Effie eventually broke down in tears of frustration and said just what she thought of the unprofessional attitude of both of them, and the Greek system in general. Whether it was what she said, or the fact that she had been reduced to tears, we don't know but by the next morning Spyros had produced a working format for us to give to Lakis who, in turn, within the day, produced the pieces of paper we had been asking for for nearly two weeks. These were cleared by the tax office and sent away to be published in the Company Gazette in Athens. Spyros assured us that it would be unlikely to take more than a month to come through, but for the moment we could go no further.

It was during this nerve racking period that Effie's mother in England, preparing to move house, was becoming more and more pressing in her demands that Effie go back and help. But, as a shareholder in our Company, Effie was required to sign all documents on the day of the purchase in Ioannina, so she had to be on hand. All we could say was that we would do our best, but we were not prepared to lose our house now on the strength of her move. And then, to crown it all, Mr. Ferandinos, who had been under no obligation to produce a single document, announced he was growing impatient!

Towards the end of Spyros' projected month we called his office daily for news of the Gazette. Negative answers played on our nerves and an anxious Eleni was batting excuses to an ever impatient Ferandinos. In desperation we decided to play ahead of the game and made a firm date to sign the papers in Ioannina. All being well this should take place in two weeks time on the morning of the Friday. To pacify her mother, Effie booked a ticket for the flight from Corfu to England for the following Monday.

Not until the Tuesday of that fateful week did we hear from Spyros that he had the Gazette in his possession but, it would have to be testified by a notary who was unavailable until Thursday morning. Thursday morning!

We had planned to go over to Ioannina on Thursday and spend the night in an hotel to make absolutely sure we were on the spot for our Friday appointment. This was cutting it fine to say the least. And then Spyros dropped another bombshell by saying he couldn't act for us on the mainland. In Greece, he said, lawyers are only allowed to act within their own canton. Eleni would be there with two Ioanninan lawyers but without Spyros, whose English was impeccable, we were going to feel very vulnerable amongst so many non-English speaking strangers. We mentioned this to Pippa, a friend of long standing, and she kindly volunteered to act as our translator and come with us. She was fascinated to see the house and had business in Ioannina anyway. We would all go together in her car and she would meet us down at the port at 1.30pm after our appointment with the notary.

Greece is still very much a cash society and we had to pay Ferandinos in drachmas and carry enough extra to pay the lawyers, notary, taxes and stamp duties. At the bank we withdrew £8,000 amounting to some 2,000,000 drachmas. Considering the highest value banknote then was 5000 drachmas, by the time I had stuffed all my pockets with wads of money I left looking something like the Michelin Man. I would have been highly nervous doing this in England, but in Greece it's not unusual to see people carrying around such sums of money and I've never heard of anyone being set upon and robbed.

Thursday came. At ten in the morning we met in Spyros' office. He was in a jovial mood probably, I suspect, cheered by the thought that we were going to the mainland and would, at last, be off his back. Formalities at the notary over, and with time on our hands, we stopped at the Gallery Inn for a quick drink. The locals had suffered the ups and downs of our saga all these years and it was for them almost as exciting a day as it was for us. With their farewells and good lucks, we left to meet Pippa at the port.

It was chaotic! Foot passengers were struggling with suitcases and paper parcels, juggernauts fumed diesel, there were buses, coaches, cars and people everywhere. We spotted Pippa, waving our tickets in the air, beside her car near the beginning of a haphazard queue waiting to drive onto the ferry. As we chatted in the sunshine telling her how our day had gone so far, all at once a terrific scuffle broke out behind us. Men were shouting and pushing each other, gesticulating with threatening fists and stamping feet. A hat was thrown down in challenge, the crowd got bigger and everyone joined in. Sirens blaring, blue lights flashing, two Port Police jeeps swept round the corner and screeched to a halt. Smartly gaitered, pistol-packing policemen strode into the fray. Failing to quell the crowd they arrested six men at random, pushed them into the jeeps and screeched away, tyres smoking. What on earth was going on?

Pippa went over to talk to some of the men involved and came back with the news that the loaders had called a lightning strike so there'd be no more ferries today. Unbelievable! To think we had come so far, through the past two months and now, at the very last minute - A FERRY STRIKE! We were dumbfounded. Pippa had noticed another ferry, four down the line from us, which seemed to be loading, and she turned and disappeared leaving us rooted to the spot. Ten minutes later she was back, clutching a new wad of tickets.

"Quick!" she said, "I'll explain later!" and we fell into the car. We were facing in the wrong direction but managed to turn against a tidal wave of disorder and literally fought our way to the other ferry. There were no loaders - this was a free for all. A huge articulated lorry was slowly jackknifing backwards onto the boat. A small Fiat decided to squeeze in behind and with a graunch of metal, the corner of the trailer ripped open the top of the car as easily as a can opener. We didn't wait to see the outcome because the accident gave us the slot we needed. Pippa shot up the ramp and we were on!

From the safety of the upper deck we looked down on a scene of utter confusion. The Captain, who had been watching it all with a semi-amused expression, decided enough was enough. He blasted the ship's horn loud and long and gave orders to cast off. Even as the hydraulic ramp started to lift, a terrier of a car had a go at jumping aboard. The ferry moved away and we were free from the jetty. The Bar beckoned.

"What in heaven's name was that all about?" I asked Pippa.

In the past, Pippa had run excursions from Corfu to archaeological sites on the mainland and had got to know the various captains on the ferry boats. The Captain of this one was a notorious flirt. He had a new girlfriend in Igoumenitsa and to be with her he was breaking the strike. The crisis of being stranded in Corfu, unable to get to Ioannina in time, had been averted by an affair of the heart! Our mental image of the girlfriend in Igoumenitsa made Helen of Troy fade into insignificance.

We stayed at the Olympic Hotel in the centre of Ioannina. As arranged, Eleni met us in the foyer next morning and together we trooped off to the notary. On the brink of actually buying the house, we were beginning to suffer from a distinct attack of cold feet and it didn't help to find that the notary's office was a buzzing hive of activity, typewriters pounding away, urgent phone calls being made, lawyers arguing, small points being added to our contract, others taken out. Pippa was verbally translating each sheet of the contract as they came hot off the press. In the middle of this bedlam, Mr. Ferandinos arrived, a tall man with groomed grey hair wearing something akin to a de-mob suit and over it, despite the warmth of the day, a thick black coat which came down to his ankles. His electric blue eyes scanned the office and came to rest on us.

"Are you German?" he barked.

"English!" I replied, offering my passport as proof. He waved it aside.

"As you are English it is all right. To a German I will not sell."

He turned, sat down, lit a cigarette and in a half trance settled himself to wait.

Between translating, Pippa found time to explain that during the war the Germans had burned and ransacked many of the villages in Zagoria, destroying homes, killing livestock, impoverishing families. Villagers were taken away and summarily shot. Lists of their names were displayed in the local kafeneons for all to see. The older people who had suffered at their hands would consider it a shameful act of betrayal for anyone to sell their house to a German.

After an hour, the contracts were ready. Our 'topographico' was laid out on the notary's desk and the multitudinous sheets spread over it, each one of which had to be signed by Effie and me, Pippa as translator, Mr. Ferandinos, and the notary. A tedious business. Finally the notary asked for the money which I extracted from all the various pockets about my person, half expecting to produce a stray white rabbit. The notary and one of the lawyers counted it. It was stacked and pushed across to Mr.

Ferandinos who opened his coat and packed the bundles into a cavernous pocket in the lining. This he fastened securely with two gigantic nappy pins and the coat was closed round him with the finality of a vault door.

Would it be possible, Mr. Ferandinos asked, if we could pay for his expenses.

"How much?"

Considering our own expenses, the topographico, multitudes of lawyers and notaries, we were aghast. Twenty thousand drachmas was the figure he suggested, about £80...

"What! For the bus ride from Igoumenitsa to Ioannina and back?" interjected the notary.

"And my time."

We felt rather sorry for this man who, now that he knew we were English, had spotted a source to be tapped, and we paid up.

Would it be possible if he could have the garden benches still in the house? He'd made them himself.

The notary stared in disbelief.

"No it would not!" he exclaimed without referring to us. "You have just signed away any rights you have to the house and its contents. You've got your money so off you go home before I lose my temper!"

Mr. Ferandinos said nothing, shook my hand and quietly left.

The last we saw of him he was boarding the bus for Igoumenitsa, laden down with bulging bags of shopping, purchased no doubt with his expenses.

The deed was done and we were the proud owners of a house in Zagoria at last. We longed to go straight up to Koukouli and see it but Pippa suggested that we ought first to find out what the ferry situation was. A phone call to

Igoumenitsa revealed that we had caught the last ferry out of Corfu yesterday and it would be the only one returning, at five o'clock. To catch it we were advised to be there in good time. So we grabbed a hasty lunch and fled for Igoumenitsa.

We certainly owed it to Pippa for getting us to Ioannina against the odds and now for getting us back, but it did seem strange not to have seen the house. After all the events leading to the purchase it felt flat somehow. Never mind, there were plenty of days ahead so maybe it didn't matter after all. I stood at the window in Paleomagaza when we got home and looked across at the snow capped mountains and, rather smugly, I thought to myself, "We've bloody well done it!"

It was late April, the time for us to be getting all the houses and pools ready for the summer, but we snatched occasional weekends off and, camping in one of the rooms in the larger house, did battle with the stinging nettles, bagged up rubbish, lit bonfires and met up with the neighbours. Curiosity and cups of coffee appeared over the garden wall. Plates of snacks came, with nods of satisfaction at what we were doing. With the garden roughly cleared we could stand back and see that we had quite a sizeable plot, large by Zagorian standards. The two houses certainly looked happier, and we had measured and doodled out plans for them. The smaller would be for us, with a kitchen and bathroom downstairs, the bathroom actually under the stairs. The first floor, which was bigger, would make a lovely living room with a bedroom leading off at a slightly lower level. By restructuring the roofline we could squeeze a small mezzanine floor over part of the bedroom, just enough for a study.

A site meeting was held in the middle of summer with Eleni and Mitsos, her builder. Mitsos was fortyish, with a round, sunny face as tanned as a nut. He spoke no English but our Greek, out of necessity and the desire to communicate, had come on apace and our vocabulary was peppered with building terms. Mitsos had a heavy work schedule restoring other houses in the area but he would be able to begin on ours, he thought, by the beginning of September. Meanwhile, Eleni would interpret our doodles into acceptable plans and go about obtaining all the necessary permits and licences.

September soon arrived and on one of our weekend visits we discovered on site a cement mixer, scaffolding, planking, tools and a mini bulldozer just narrow enough to negotiate village streets. This was impressively professional since most Greek builders, in our experience at least, seemed to own not a single tool, expecting their clients to provide everything.

At the site meeting it had been thought that only one wall would have to be pulled down, but now we were told that the south facing wall with the fireplace in it needed to come down as well. This was disturbing news, so early in the day. I have an inbuilt suspicion of architects and builders; they are, to me, similar to Advertising Agents inasmuch as they love spending other people's money. We were working to a budget, a word that doesn't appear in their vocabulary. I began to get nervous. It seemed that all the questions we had asked on site to which the answer had been, 'no problem', were, after all, going to cost. So we came over to find out what it was all about. From what we saw it was clear the wall would, indeed, have to be rebuilt but the cost was not going to be as bad as I had feared. We gave Mitsos the go-ahead and left him to it. But we decided we would make monthly visits to check on progress and make sure that neither the builders, nor the added costs, ran away with themselves.

Building a house anywhere is no easy matter, but building in Greece halfway up a mountain by remote control from Corfu is quite another thing, and our next visit was filled with apprehension. Would Mitsos be there? Would any work have been done? We turned the corner in the lane. The wrought iron gates and the walls to which they had been attached were gone. The south facing wall had come down and was back up, butting against the sky, proud as a peacock in what must have been its original glory. The other wall, the one we had known about, was also back up and three new walls for our bedroom were nearly finished. It was staggering the speed at which the work had been done when you consider we're talking about stone walls over two feet thick! The next stage would be to get the roof on. Ours was not a large roof, but it was going to require heavy timbering. The stone slates alone would weigh over ten tons and allowance had to be made for the weight of a possible metre of snow.

Mitsos showed us how the main timbers would be specially cut to interlock and how, basically, the entire superstructure was counterbalanced, and held itself together. Over this, boarding was laid, on top of that, sheet metal, then more boarding and finally the stone slabs. This was the traditional way of building these stone roofs, apart from the modern usage of sheet metal which serves both to rainproof and insulate the end result. Mitsos is a third generation builder and it was obvious he knew what he was about. We were filled with confidence in his skills and... by our next visit we had a roof! Inside in the living room and bedroom all those beams, king pins, and joists were revealed. In most of the old houses we had seen all this would have been concealed above wooden ceilings but we decided to leave ours open. It was attractive as a feature and added height and a sense of airiness to the rooms.

The time had come for the electrician to do his bit. I had already drawn up a plan of where we wanted all the various sockets, light fixtures and so on. It hadn't been easy, not having lived in the house, not knowing our final layout or how we would arrange the furniture, but we reckoned we'd got it about right. In Greece they favour the continental way of wiring, all around the tops of walls with small, round plastic discs covering the junction boxes. Sometimes these are installed in unsightly clusters and one wall can have five or more of the things. Invariably the discs curl up and drop off exposing a gaping hole with a snarl of coloured wires in it, and it's impossible to get a replacement disc to stay put. I hated them. We asked the electrician if he couldn't do our wiring the English way, at skirting board level. He wasn't sure. It was a new idea to him, he'd never been asked to wire a house in this way and he'd have to check with the Electricity Board to see if they approved the system. Fortunately they did, and having undertaken the work he made an excellent job of it. The plumber had installed basic waste pipes before the floors were laid and the rest would follow.

In February we went over to find the house in two feet of snow and all work at a halt. But we were pleased to see the window frames were in and that the end bedroom wall, built into the banking, which Mitsos had specially waterproofed, was bone dry. Plastering and final bits still had to be done, but inside the house was already beginning to look larger and more spacious than we had imagined. Spring was round the corner and we had no real worries about the completion.

One evening in Corfu, our landlord paid us a visit. He had a problem. His son and daughter-in-law, who lived in Athens, had decided to come back and live and work on Corfu. They wanted the house. This in itself did not come as a surprise since anyone living in rented property knew they were in danger of losing it once they had made improvements. We had seen it happen so often. What was surprising was its happening to us now, all of eight years after we first moved in. We'd been lucky to have such a long run.

This uncertainty of living in rented accommodation had been an important factor in our decision to go ahead and buy a larger house in Zagoria and re-route our lives. Also, after several years living on Corfu during which we had only visited our cottage in Cornwall twice, we had begun to feel there was little point in hanging on to it. We'd kept a few sentimental treasures, most of which we had with us in Paleomagaza, and sold everything else. We couldn't envisage returning to live permanently in England so better to have the finance to buy in Greece. Not in Corfu where prices are astronomical; the same, we were told by a disillusioned American, as buying on Manhattan Island. But we needed something to call our own. Thank heavens we had persevered and made our investment in Zagoria. I asked Spyros the obvious question,

"When?"

"As soon as possible."

I explained that we were planning to move to our house in Koukouli but that wouldn't be until September when work on it was finished. They could have Paleomagaza then. With arms outstretched in a gesture of goodwill he said he was happy to have us stay as long as we wanted, but he was under pressure from his family. They needed it sooner. Could we, perhaps, think about it?

The thinking we did was to go to Spyros the lawyer. On Corfu there are such a number of Spyros that to avoid confusion they're usually referred to by what they are, as in 'Spyros the lawyer', 'Spyros the landlord', 'Spyros the kafeneon', and so forth. From Spyros the lawyer we learned that, because we had rented the house for such a long time, had paid unfailingly, and maintained the property at our own expense, we were bomb - and landlord - proof. Technically there was nothing the landlord could do to get us to leave, and if he tried to play silly games by taking us to court, Spyros the lawyer could spin the whole thing out for as long as was needed. At least we knew where we stood. When the landlord reappeared some days later, we explained our position more fully and he agreed with the lawyer's opinion. He left to tell his son there could be no house until September.

In the meantime we were continuing with our business and trying to find a buyer for it, not looking for vast sums of money but wanting to find someone reliable to take it over. This we managed to do, a modest sum was paid, we handed over our contracts and were happy that, like Jim before us, we had not let our clients down.

Mr. Biffet, the dog, was another problem that had to be sorted. We'd found him two years before in a client's garage, a whimpering, frightened puppy - dumped. Against my better judgement, but egged on by Effie's pathetic expression when she picked him up to comfort him, he had come to live with us. He grew and grew, and grew. A keen gardener was Mr. Biffet. Geraniums he dug up by the dozen, new shoots were severely cut back, not a flower pot was left unturned and he was very partial to petunias. Nothing was left unchewn: shoes, chair legs, cook books, the newspaper, swimming things left out to dry; anything to keep himself amused. He was, for all that, a very loving and lovable dog. Our main worry was that, having lived all his life within the confines of Paleomagaza, we had no idea what his reaction would be faced with the free range chicken, sheep and goats of a Zagorian village. We couldn't risk moving into Koukouli with a dog who might go about chewing up the villagers' livestock! A home had to be found for him on Corfu. And it had to be someone who really liked and wanted him, someone who would accept him as part of the family, which is what he had become with us. We couldn't bear to think of him chained to an overturned, rusty barrel in a trash filled chicken run with nothing but the hens and local sparrows for company. But who? Who could we ask to take him?

"What about Vasilis?"

"Vasilis said he would never have another dog after Toby died."

"Yes, I know, but that was over two years ago..."

We approached Jo, his wife. She would love a dog, it would be good for the children to grow up with one, but she couldn't be sure about Vasilis. The best thing would be for him to meet Mr. Biffet. If he fell for the dog, then perhaps he'd change his mind, so we invited them up for drinks one evening.

Mr. Biffet put on a star performance. It was perfect, Oscar-winning stuff. He looked up at Vasilis with his big, loving eyes, gently took crisps from his hand and as gently asked for another with his paw. He rested his chin on Vasilis' knee. It was pathetic.... but at the end of the evening Vasilis had agreed they would take him. We were overjoyed! They lived by the sea, had a large garden and Mr. Biffet would live 'en famille'. On our first visit back to Corfu we stayed with Jo and Vasilis and found Mr. Biffet, lying on the sofa, feet in the air, watching television with the two small children piled round him. He was in seventh heaven.

Moving in

The cat had been moping about the house like a surly teenager for the past week or more, eyeing and sitting on the growing mound of cardboard boxes slowly being amassed in the living room. Batty had been fobbed off on us by some well meaning person when we first came to Corfu. She was beautifully marked, with an adorable face but we were to discover that she was, without doubt, the most unlovable, disagreeable cat ever created. If, and 'if' was debatable, she condescended to honour you with her presence and sit on your lap, it was only passing seconds before she had taken a large and painful lump out of your hand. By arrangement with the landlord's son, Nikos, and his wife Mary, Batty was to remain at Paleomagaza. I had told her this, from a distance of course, and perhaps that was why she had such a disdainful gleam in her eye.

Tonight was to be our last in Paleomagaza, our home for eight happy and enjoyable years. Sitting under the verandah, the evening sun turning the sky a kaleidoscope of colours, we watched, as we had a thousand times before, the swallows swoop and dive. Any minute now they would cease to be swallows and become bats instead. With a glass of wine and the air filled with the headiness of night scented jessamine, it was a moment for quiet reflection. The old house was all but empty, with Mr. Biffet settled in his new home. Time, it seemed, stood still.

The distant BOOM of a disco shattered the illusion - Corfu night-life in all its shoddiness, let loose on an otherwise tranquil evening. Corfu had been good to us and we had lived here with no regrets and many friends made. But now the noise, the ever spreading concrete blocks, the destruction of olive groves, roads bulldozed down to once secret beaches, caique tripper boats blaring out the latest pop; the old town overrun with jewellery shops, boutiques and trash souvenir shops, the tin smiths, lampmakers and skilled crafts forced out by escalating rents - Corfu had sold its soul to cheap tourism. The time had come to leave.

Mitsos, our master-builder, had volunteered to come and help us move. At ten the following morning his truck rattled up our drive. We had already packed Suzi, and on previous runs had taken the washing machine and fridge. He surveyed what was left, worked out the shapes like a Mensa test candidate and together we loaded. By having the tailgate down and using some moth-eaten rope, we succeeded in getting the last two garden chairs on board. With a final look round, a pat of thanks on the door, closing it for the last time, and Batty conspicuous by her absence, we set off in convoy for the port.

As the season was nearly over, the ferry was almost empty and Mitsos parked his truck in the middle of the deck in a strategic position for driving off. These island ferryboats have a strong similarity to flat bottomed punts or landing craft, the idea being that in times of national crisis the Greek Military can usefully commandeer them. Viewed from the top deck, Mitsos' truck looked like a Dinky toy. And sticking out of it at all angles were all our worldly goods, things that we loved and needed, reduced to nothing more than a lorry load of seemingly useless junk.

As the ferry noisily vibrated its way through the flat,

calm sea, we went down to the Saloon to while away the time. There, over the engines, the noise was tremendous, and the juddering so great that pop bottles in the cooler clattered and clinked against each other. The television was blaring, space invader machines bleeped and an espresso machine hissed. It was impossible to read, the print danced up and down, and you put your coffee cup on the table top at risk of having it land in your lap. We ordered toasties, and ate them propping ourselves up against the cafeteria counter. Barely warm, wrapped round with a paper serviette that partially stuck to them and had to be eaten, they turned out to consist of a veneer of ham and a condom-thin slice of cheese between compressed slabs of sweet, butterless toast. This was standard catering on the island ferries and never varied from one to the other.

It was insufficient fodder for Mitsos so, halfway to Zagoria, we stopped at a small roadside taverna Effie and I had discovered on early house hunting trips. The owners had a smallholding and produced incredible amounts of vegetables, pulses, wine, chipero and feta cheese. They ground their own maize, gathered a countless variety of herbs and sold eggs fresh from the nest. Nowhere could you find a tastier omelette and salad.

Once in Koukouli, we went on ahead in Suzi and waited for Mitsos to back up as far as he could into the village. We were at the bottom of our little lane which was steep and winding. It was going to be an awful job manhandling everything up. But, urged on by Mitsos, who had been chugging up and down in his bobcat for months, I found that with a few tactical twitches of the steering wheel I could just get Suzi to the house. If only we'd known that when we brought over the washing machine! So we shuttled back and forth loading Suzi from the lorry. Papa

Kostas and his family poured out of their house at the first sign of activity and lent a multitude of hands. Once everything was stacked safely inside, Mitsos left, refusing any form of payment, not even for petrol money or the cost of the ferry. It was, he said, his housewarming present.

We were alone in our own home in Zagoria, a home that we owned, lock, stock and barrel. It felt marvellous. It looked like a bomb site with boxes, furniture, everything, dumped at random. We'd been invited to supper by Papa Kostas and, tired though we were, it was obvious we were expected and would have to go. The boxes could all be sorted tomorrow, the most important thing was to assemble and make the bed. Sitting on the edge of it, the only comfortable place to sit, we had a celebratory tot of chipero and afterwards I went downstairs to wash and freshen up. It was then I discovered that we didn't appear to have any water. I had noticed, in passing, a white flexible pipe fitted to our main stop cock which seemed to disappear over the wall in the direction of our neighbour's garden. Following it now some hundred yards over nettles and briars I found it was mysteriously connected to his garden standpipe. As I was fiddling with the tap to see if anything happened, he came shambling up.

Petros is a man in his mid-fifties, with a large hooked nose and close set eyes. He was wearing a massively peaked baseball cap in a garish yellow, which added considerably to his already vulture-like features. I explained that we didn't have any water and pointed hopefully to the pipe. Petros is asthmatic, a nervous and excitable man who speaks with a stutter, and it was difficult to understand quite what he was on about. The bit I did make out was that none of the village had water at this time of the year, except for half an hour a day between 9.30 and

10 in the morning. If we needed some now we could fill a bucket at one of the springs by the church. Well, that at least was something, and the church wasn't very far away.

We found a bucket and some empty plastic bottles and walked to the springs. Behind the church, and built onto it, there is a run of beautiful arched buildings that climb the hillside. The upper floor originally comprised the old school rooms and two little grace and favour dwellings, one each for the village priest and teacher. Underneath are the lofty, arched wellhouses through which the cobbled way passes, and from amongst mossed walls and old carved stones five springs flow continually. The water was ice cold and tasted divine. Whisky and this, I thought, are going to prove fine companions.

That evening, we packed ourselves for the second time into Papa Kostas' little kitchen, wood-burning stove at full throttle and the three boys ranged down one side of the table like a set of jugs. Kiki, their only daughter and the eldest, saw that everyone had something to drink, and Papa Kostas' wife, Elevtheria, laid out the food. There was egg-lemon soup with chunks of bread straight out of the oven, feta from her father's sheep, tasty knobbly tomatoes and pickled green chillies, all supplemented with the Papas' own homemade wine, a tangy sparkling rosé. Kiki, who shyly spoke a little schoolgirl English, helped us to communicate but both Papa Kostas and Elevtheria seemed quick to grasp what we were trying to put across, and the evening was jolly and informal. Walking back to our house under a clear, starry sky, with their cheery 'goodnights' following us up the lane, I had an overwhelming feeling of contentment. Sleep would close a magical day.

In the middle of the night we were both woken by a vibrant, metallic 'pinging' noise, just outside the bedroom window. We waited, ears straining. Here there were no discos, no nearby arterial roads, no one out and about in the early hours of the morning. The silence was absolute. 'Ping!', it happened again. Not too willingly I went outside with a torch to investigate. I moved closer to where the sound had come from. 'Ping', and then PLONK! - right on the top of my head making me jump out of my skin! But the mystery was solved. I was standing under a walnut tree on a scrap of land with a small, tin-roofed shed on it. At night-time, in Koukouli, the noise of a walnut landing onto a tin roof sounds much like a rifle shot in your back garden.

Those first days were spent sorting ourselves out. The house had been finished to a rough stage: the walls were raw stucco; the kitchen only had a sink in it; the bathroom a bath, basin and loo. There were no cupboards and nothing had been painted. All this sort of finishing off we intended to do ourselves during the winter. As there were no balustrades on the stairwell in the living room, we piled boxes around to stop anybody inadvertently dropping over the edge. Temporarily, I nailed a wooden pole against the beams in the mezzanine and we hung clothes there. Boxes with kitchen things went into the kitchen and the rest we put into storage in the other building.

People in the village came to introduce themselves and see how we were settling in. It was natural they should be intrigued to see how two English people could cope with moving into a half finished house with severe water rationing. They could not have realised that on Corfu water is scarce, and we had learned what a precious commodity it is; we were used to coping with shortages. But they never came empty handed, bringing gifts of pies, eggs, potatoes, home-made wine, preserves and flowers. Our potted plants had been left with friends on Corfu but within days we had pots of chrysanthemums, petunias, geraniums, roses and basil. We were touched by their generosity and especially by the gift from Elevtheria of basil which, in Greece, is looked upon as a talisman bringing you health, long life and good fortune.

It was urged upon us by our visitors that we must, in return, visit them. It would have been churlish not to do so and anyway it's lovely being invited into other people's houses. There are so many fascinating things to be seen, especially in these old village houses. So, apart from trips to Ioannina to get basic shopping and two large plastic containers for storing some of our half hour share of water, we were unexpectedly caught up in a social whirl.

The population of Koukouli in the summer months grows to about sixty. People living in towns and cities migrate to the village to spend the hottest months in houses they have, for the most part, inherited. Many had already returned home by the time we arrived, their houses shut up for the winter, so we weren't aware of the situation and were rather surprised to be constantly asked: "When are you leaving?"

We explained that we had only just arrived.

"Yes, yes. But you'll be leaving before winter, won't you?"

They had assumed we were 'summer people'. Not an unusual assumption when you consider the great number of Greeks with second homes, and with our being English they automatically took it we had a house in England. We assured them that we had no other house, we had come to live in Koukouli permanently. They tut-tutted in disbelief and you could tell from their expression they didn't expect to find us here next year. But news in a village travels fast and we quickly learned that we had won an enormous amount of street credibility with the fifteen permanent villagers, the 'winter people'.

One day, busy in the house, to our surprise a tannoy burst into action close by. Like British Rail tannoys, the voice sounded as though it came from the bottom of a bucket but I thought I recognised it as Petros. A loud 'click' terminated the announcement and immediately a dog set up with the most bloodcurdling howls! We stood looking at each other. What was going on? It turned out I was right about it being Petros. He and his wife Maria were official keepers of the one village telephone. Whenever someone rang, Petros or Maria, in whose house the phone was installed, answered and then put out a call over the tannoy for the person who was wanted. Obviously, for people who lived across the village the caller was asked to phone back in ten minutes, giving them time to be in situ, but not in our case, living next door. Whenever we heard our names called we dropped everything, ran down the garden, over the wall, through Petros' chicken run, past the outhouses, across their courtyard and through the door into the hallway, where the phone sat in pride of place on a table covered with mock lace oilskin. We would arrive utterly breathless and quite unable to speak.

It may seem rather quaint to people who accept the telephone as an accessory to everyday life, but for the villagers the system was perfect. You could be anywhere, out in the fields, visiting, or loafing around in the village plateia and you would know if there was a call for you. The tannoy was also useful to fetch someone home if they were out and about or to announce oncoming water rationing or electricity strikes. The howling was Lucy, a dog belonging to two elderly spinster sisters. Lucy absolutely loathed the sound of the tannoy and never failed to tune in after a call.

October was a glorious month, but a sense of winter approaching could not be dismissed. Out in the woodlands villagers were collecting sweet chestnuts by the sackful. Walnut gathering was at its peak and everyone seemed to be up trees lashing them with long poles in a frenzy to bring down the last nut. The village echoed to the sound of this flailing and nuts dropping in showers. We had a walnut tree in the garden. No doubt before our arrival the walnuts were scrumped, but now they were ours and we gathered them as they fell. Never having owned a walnut tree before, we cracked the nuts and stored the kernels in jars ready for Christmas. What we should have done, so we learned, was lay them out to dry for a month or more and then crack them open. By Christmas, ours were green with mould.

Petros and Maria had invited us for coffee. Maria is a slight, energetic woman then in her late forties, with a mischievous face full of fun, who never stops working from dawn to dusk. We sat in their flower filled courtyard and she served us little cups of black, thick coffee, glasses of cold water and, on cut-glass saucers, a sweet preserve. This was traditional hospitality wherever you visited. The sweetmeats or 'glyka', were usually made from plums, cherries, melon, or some local grown fruit. Maria gave us what, from the look of it, I took to be prunes. I cut into one with a teaspoon. It was soft as butter and tasted delicious but it was not a prune. Maria was watching me with twinkling eyes. Did I know what it was? I had no idea. It was a walnut! She told us how they pick the walnuts early, around June, before the shell has hardened, and for a month soak them in water changing it every day. Then they boil them for hours with sugar before bottling the end result. It's a long and bothersome, not to mention messy, process, and to be given a jar as a present is an honour indeed.

There were other signs of the changing seasons. Maria was seen setting off into the woodlands with a small handsaw and a coil of home plaited rope, reappearing bent double under a bush of freshly hacked shrubbery lashed to her back, winter feed for the sheep and goats. Logs materialised, neatly stacked in outhouses, stove pipes were brought out and banged and bashed to dislodge last year's carbon deposits; gardens were pruned, vegetable plots dug over and manured, and potted plants moved indoors. This communal participation in the seasonal activities of mountain survival was a new experience for us, and we realised that little could have changed over centuries.

One of our first tasks had been to paint all the outside windows before the onset of bad weather. We also needed to buy a larger fridge freezer, something big enough to be serviceable when we were running the hotel because, once that was installed, we could get on with designing the layout of the kitchen. Eleni referred us to a paintshop in Ioannina run by three very helpful and well meaning men and we were soon equipped with paint, brushes, thinners, masking tape and scrapers. The fridge freezer was a more expensive and more difficult purchase. We wandered for miles around Ioannina comparing prices, sizes, shapes and special features, getting more and more confused, ending up back at the little shop we'd started from. There we had seen a German model which had that clean, German no-nonsense look about it. Height and depth were exactly what we were looking for to fit into the kitchen and maximise on space. The price tag said 250,000 drachmas. Expensive, but then all electrical goods in Greece were.

"Is that the price?" we asked the young salesman, glumly. He looked at the tag, then at us.

"No," he said. "I give you another price"

With the aid of a pocket calculator he arrived at the figure of 190,000 drachmas. This was getting more interesting but before we went any further I thought I had better explain where we lived and find out whether he could deliver the monster. Quite unfazed at having to drive the twenty five miles to Koukouli and then back, he said he knew the village and would meet us by the church at seven o'clock that evening. We paid and were given a receipt and left, slightly dazed by the speed and ease of the transaction.

We had had some appalling experiences on Corfu when buying appliances. Either the shop failed repeatedly to deliver when they said they would, or they delivered the wrong item. There was never any paperwork and a guarantee lasted until the moment their van disappeared down the drive. So, I was more than a little apprehensive when I turned up at the plateia at a quarter to seven to look out for our fridge.

The kafeneon was open. Petros and Maria ran it, in addition to being keepers of the phone, in charge of delivering post, and responsible for monitoring the village water. They seemed absolutely tireless. I ordered a chipero from Petros and we stood together in the doorway, chatting. I was beginning to understand him better, despite his nervous stutter, and had warmed to his mild sense of humour and his straightforwardness. We heard the sound of a car approaching. So few come to the village that it is possible to spend days without hearing a single one. When you do hear one it's quite an event. This event, to my relief, was the arrival of our fridge. A massive, macho, 4 x 4 pick up truck with polished hi-tech chrome wheels backed into the village. Helped by a couple of shepherds from the kafeneon, between us we managed to hump the fridge freezer up to the house, and within minutes it stood in the middle of our kitchen in its cardboard packaging, like some monolith from outer space.

I've long been of the opinion that women are very much better at painting than men - a belief that has saved me hours of tedious work. So it was cheering to see that Effie was making steady progress with the outside windows, up and down ladders dropping the sandpaper and having to break off to make countless cups of coffee. My temporary workshop, set up in the nearest room of the other building, was in some sort of workable order and I was ready to start fitting out the bathroom with wooden panelling to conceal the internal, wall mounted, water-pipes.

Ioannina is recognised as the timber centre of Greece and woodcarving and woodturning are predominant. We had spotted many timber yards on our shopping trips but I needed to find one that would cut and plane my timber more or less to size. I spent a weary morning going from one to another but either they couldn't understand my Greek or were unwilling to cut such small amounts. On my way home, defeated, I remembered there was a massive timber yard, out of Ioannina, on the left. Maybe I should give them a try? Not that I held out much hope since the smaller merchants had dismissed me, but maybe they'd know of another who might help.

There was a large, hanger-like building from which I heard the sharp whining of woodworking machinery. Inside, men were feeding a great, green contraption with raw planks and tongued and grooved boards were coming out the other end. A thumping great fan drew the sawdust off through huge, slinky silver piping overhead, to a vast hopper outside. It looked like a highly professional outfit. The noise was appalling. A tall young man in his mid-thirties, wearing jeans and leather braces, approached me. Over the din I asked if he spoke English.

"Yes I do," he shouted back. "And if you want, I can convert metres into feet and inches, rods, poles or perches!" and with a broad grin he nodded his head to indicate we should go outside to talk.

Crossing the yard to the offices, he introduced himself. His name was Apostolis and he was the general manager of the family owned business which had been started by his grandfather. In the offices he handed me a large whisky and pouring one for himself explained that the company specialised in the making of floorboards, ceiling boards and cornicings, as well as carrying a substantial stock of plywoods, conti-boards and MDF. It was impressive. I told him about our houses and what I was after, and asked if he knew of anyone who'd be able to help me. He did. He, Apostolis, would be happy to cut any wood to size no matter how big or small the order. My problem was solved, and with his command of English I could look forward to being able to talk timber with a man who knew his business.

The following day, towards evening, he turned up at the house with a bottle of whisky under his arm and a bunch of flowers for Effie.

"Curiosity got the better of me," he explained. "I just had to come and find out what you were up to." He stayed for dinner and a lasting friendship was formed.

Many of the villages in Zagoria have forestry rights and a specified amount of timber, mainly oak, can be cut for use on the villagers' stoves during the winter. The Vlachs, a semi-nomadic tribe from Eastern Zagoria, have, for centuries, provided mule trains, once the only form of transport in the region. They cut the wood and rope it in bundles, eight feet long, on either side of the mules, tied to a specially made wooden saddle. Sometimes as many as twenty mules will descend from the mountains and arrive in the village square where eager customers barter for the logs, sold by the mule load. The laden beasts patiently stand in line, heads hanging, until led to the purchaser's house. There the Vlach leader tweaks the ropes tied to the saddle, the logs clatter to the ground on either side, and the mule walks on and waits until all the loads ordered have been similarly delivered.

There are not enough people in Koukouli to warrant the arrival of the Vlach, but most of the winter people own pockets of woodland and cut from there. We were not in this fortunate position, so would have to go down to the valley and buy our logs from the logman on the main road. Papa Kostas had a twenty year old Toyota pick-up and volunteered to fetch a couple of tons for us before the onset of cold weather. One morning we set off together in the truck, Papa Kostas in his black cassock with his stove pipe hat firmly planted on his head, driving, as all Papasses do, at breakneck speed with God on their side. The clutch was let out and we leapt forward like a kicked dog, lurching down the road, the steering wheel twitching and shaking of its own accord. It became clear to me after a few hundred yards that the much battered truck had some serious and dangerous mechanical faults. The dashboard suddenly vibrated violently as Papa Kostas savagely applied the well worn brakes, and cigarette packets, pens, old combs and notepads fell to the floor.

Uphill, the going was not so frightening but

downhill it was terrifying, the truck gathering added momentum aided by gravity. Faster and faster we sped, twisting bends came and went, the mountain edge crept closer and dropped forever, the entire truck shook and rattled. Approaching a blind corner, Papa Kostas decided that this was the moment to hunt for his cigarette packet, now lying somewhere in the car well. I was too speechless to offer help - the whites of my knuckles warning me to concentrate on holding on! If I hadn't believed in God when we started, I was a total convert by the time we arrived.

The logman, introduced by Papa Kostas, proudly showed me some ferocious looking splitting machines which he said he had constructed himself and judging by missing fingers on his hand, it was obvious that a considerable amount of research and development had gone into their making. Totally overloaded, the truck, Papa Kostas and I attacked the mountain road for the return journey. Fortunately for my shattered nerves, this was a more leisurely trip, uphill with two tons of logs on board. But that night I had a terrible dream of sharp boomerang bends rushing at me and a Toyota flying over a precipice with the devil beside me dressed in priest's clothing, flaming logs hurtling down on us. In my new found religious state I vowed that I would never, never again drive with Papa Kostas!

Years ago on Corfu we had bought a wood-burning stove. Exported by an American company, made in Taiwan, it was a cheaper version of the Swedish Jotel stove. This international production came with us to Koukouli. Mitsos had designed and built a traditional Zagorian fireplace to take it on the hearthstone, with the pipe running directly up the chimney. The stove, we knew, was amazingly efficient; it burned slowly, used wood economically and pushed out mega therms of heat. Made of cast iron, it could be turned down to burn throughout the night without refuelling and was easily jacked up in the morning. Alone it would be sufficient to heat the living room and bedroom. The locals were not convinced. The general consensus was that the stove should be in the middle of the room, with the pipe running below the ceiling, thereby throwing off more heat. This was the method they used with their basic ex Nissen-hut stoves, as we had seen in Monodendri. Much as I appreciated the concept, I did not appreciate the idea of burning my head on a hot tin pipe every time I crossed the room, or of setting fire to our splendid rafters. Besides, our stove was efficient enough to operate without all that. It stayed where it was designed to go. Papa Kostas alone made no comment. But then, he had seen the tools and equipment set out in my temporary workshop and had probably gathered that, as a fairly practical man, I possibly knew my stove.

When the first cold snap came, our biggest doubter arrived on the doorstep early in the morning. Coffee provided, we went upstairs to the living room. He moved over to the stove, hands outstretched. "Ah ha!" he said, knowledgeably, sitting down next to it. Soon his coat came off. A few minutes later he was edging his chair away. Finally he moved altogether and sat in another chair. As he got up to leave, he nodded towards the stove.

"Kalos! Kalos!" It was a very good stove, he said, but it would be much better if it was in the middle of the room - give off more heat.

❋

After two months in Koukouli, we were still struggling with the lack of water. The novelty of bathing from a bucket in the bath was wearing thin. But by now we had found out where our water came from. Above the village at the far end from us was a small, enclosed reservoir fed by a natural spring. Because there had not been the normal winter snowfall on the mountains which, melting through the summer, keeps the springs flowing, the supply was reduced to a trickle. Add to that the influx of summer people stepping up demand and you see why there was simply not enough water to go round. Our white pipe, casually draped over the wall to Petros and Maria's standpipe, which had been transporting our precious half hour ration, would have to be properly connected and buried underground before winter came. Petros, in his role as guardian of the village water, showed us where our nearest, official, connection point was - sixty yards up the hill under the footpath by the side of our house! A trench would have to be dug from our stop cock to the mains pipe.

Later on in the morning he returned, accompanied by two itinerant, non-Greek speaking Albanians. With much bobbing of the baseball cap he gave them firm and unintelligible instructions for the digging of our trench. Their fee, he told us, for a full day's work, was their lunch, 2000 drachmas each, and a meal in the evening. Taking our pick axe and shovel, the Albanians vigorously attacked the job digging, illogically enough, from the bottom of the hill upwards.

Effie disappeared into the kitchen to rustle up some food for them, spurred on by the fact that they worked to the chant of "Polee thoulia, leega lefta, leego fagito - lots of work, little money, small meals!" - the only Greek they'd learned apart from the word for a wheelbarrow.

Within two hours they announced they'd finished and handed back the pick and shovel. I could see that the trench was nowhere near deep enough to prevent the pipes from freezing up in winter, but they stood firm, pretended not to understand, demanded their money, ate every scrap of the mountains of food Effie had prepared and left. That afternoon we started digging it out ourselves, from the top downwards, and about a foot deeper we came across a large, plastic, mains water-pipe delivering water to the lower parts of the village. It was a huge relief that the Albanians had opted out before putting the pick clean through the pipe leaving us to carry the can. At any rate, we knew we'd got to the right depth and opened the trench the whole distance. Petros and Papa Kostas, grubby in working clothes and armed with a large rusty wrench, various connectors and washers, got us properly and finally linked to the mains. We filled the trench, restored the footpath, but were still on rationed water.

A few nights later, a terrific storm burst over the village and we sat up in bed listening to the beautiful music of heavy plonking rain. The next morning a jubilant Maria came to the house to inform us that the pots and bucket days were over. We would have no water problems until next summer. At last... a bath in the evening!

Koukouli – a lifestyle

The view from our living room window leads the eye across sweeping hills covered in oak, pine, ash, chestnut and a variety of other trees, and autumn brings us an artist's palette of browns, reds, yellows and gold, highlighted by an opaline sun. As a backdrop to this fantastic display stands the snow clad ridge of Mitsikeli and way beyond, in the far distance, the sparkling peaks of Peristeri soaring to over 2000 metres.

By this time the summer people had all gone. Only the shepherds remained and soon they would be leaving too. Every year they migrate to Zagoria from Igoumenitsa, Preveza, even Arta where the grasslands, ample for their flocks in winter and spring, become scorched out of existence in the summer. Towards the middle of May huge lorries with trailers trundle up, bringing the sheep and goats travelling in three tiers. Sometimes a specially built stall attached to the back of the trailer stables two or more mules standing sideways on, nose to tail, tethered to their fenced platform, ears flattened by the slipstream. Behind the lorry will follow the shepherds' pick-up, laden with everything needed for a five month sojourn in the mountains, including their dogs. For over a week these convoys pour into the region like an arriving circus, but by Ochi Day, the 28th October, they will have left.

'Ochi' is the Greek word for 'No' and No Day is so called because it commemorates the date in 1940 when

THE PAPAS AND THE ENGLISHMAN

General Metaxas, asked by Mussolini for Greece's acquiescence to Italian troops marching through their country, replied "Ochi!" to his request. Consequently Mussolini sent 50,000 Italian troops to conquer Greece, invading the north from Albania with the intention of marching through the Pass at Kalpaki to Ioannina, and onwards to Athens. Five thousand desperately brave Greek partisans held the troops at bay. Women fought alongside men, carrying dynamite on their backs to detonate cliff sides and overhangs, blocking the passes with rock-falls. The Italian troops, prevented from moving forward and stuck in the open plain were harassed, shot at and eventually starved out. Many Greeks lost their lives but the unwavering courage of these mountain villagers in saving their country from invasion has never been forgotten. Above the modern township of Kalpaki, towering on a hilltop on lookout across the valley is the bronze replica of a partisan, gaitered, helmeted, rifle to hand and clad in the cape that was his hallmark. Vast and commanding it is a moving monument to all those Zagorians who risked and sacrificed their lives for the sake of their country. On Ochi Day, commemorated as a National Holiday, Greeks from far and wide make pilgrimage to the area and it has become customary for the shepherds to leave beforehand.

Koukouli rents out land to shepherds, on the western verge of the village. It has been rustically fenced in, a rough hut or two put up, and a concrete water catchment and trough built for the animals. Some of the shepherds, like our Mr. Ferandinos, have houses in the village for their wives and families, others camp in the huts around the corral. The men themselves set out every morning with their dogs leading the grazing flocks for miles through the countryside, returning with them in the evenings when the ewes are milked. Some shepherds, in the company of four or five mules, follow their flocks for days, even weeks, carrying their milking and cheese-making utensils with them. A hard and lonely life but it runs in these men's veins.

One shepherd we met on a warm June day, walking beside the Voidhomatis River under the coolness of a forest of leafy plane trees, had no base whatsoever. Accompanied solely by his mule which carried all his belongings - bedroll, food, ropes and the typical black cape woven from goat hair, half an inch thick and weighing a good fifteen pounds - he took his three hundred goats on a massive five month trek of Zagoria. By August they would reach the high grasslands of Astraka nearly 2,500 metres above sea level. Up there are the remains of the stone huts built by the nomadic Sarakatsani shepherds of old who spent the entire summer with their flocks on the mountain. These ancient shepherd encampments, or 'stani' as they are called, no longer in use are crumbling into decay. We tried to imagine our shepherd alone in that high wilderness of stone and windswept grass. Now he stood, hands clasped one atop the other, leaning onto his crook, watching the goats pick their way amongst the pebbles in the dappled shallows, browsing on wild mint and watercress, sunlight twinkling on water the colour of kingfisher wings. No scene could be more idyllic, more timeless or enduring. And the only sounds were of the river flowing by, accompanied by the continual melody of goat-bells.

All the goats and sheep, except for the newly born, wear bells. Made of brass or copper, worn suspended from a whittled wooden collar, each one has a different ring. The older or leader goats have great clanking copper cowbells the size of saucepans that give off a deep, distinctive base note. The rest are on an ascending scale of notes, the highest belonging to the youngest. To me, these between tones sound pretty much like one another, but a shepherd knows every animal by the sound of its bell. In Ioannina, down the shopping lanes, are a number of little shops selling nothing but bells. The old shepherds are often seen there, suited and wearing the typical flat hat usually donned for smart occasions, trying them out one by one to find exactly the timbre they want. Once chosen, the bell is weighed and paid for by the kilo.

I was sitting one evening on a grassy bank just outside the village, watching the sun set and the shadows falling between the hills. The perfect silence was broken only by the homeward symphony of a large herd moving in the distance, a pure philharmonia of four hundred bells.

The shepherds' dogs are another matter. These are a cross breed of enormous size with bear-thick fur and all have one ear docked, adding a bandit like quality to their already ferocious appearance. They are used specifically to protect the flock from predators, be they wolf or man, and are extremely dangerous if you come within their range. Their other function is to contain the animals within the grazing area and they are stationed at various outposts to chivvy any adventurers or stragglers back into the group, Quite often you come across them positioned on the road verges when the flock is nearby, and they relieve the tedium of the day by rushing out at the very last minute to attack your nearside wheel, teeth bared and barking furiously. Between the sudden shock of this onslaught and a desire not to get them under your front wheel, it makes driving a hazardous occupation.

We've spent many happy evenings at the village kafeneon sitting under the plane tree talking to the shepherds. They sit, hands clasped on their crooks or 'glitsas' as they call them, which are firmly placed on the ground between their feet. The shafts of these crooks are made from a honed branch of the Krania, a Cornelian Dogwood which grows here in profusion. Krania berries, a deep dull red, ripening in early October, were once the source of dye for the specific red of Turkish fezzes. In Zagoria now the fruit is bottled with a mixture of chipero, sugar and brandy, and left in a sunny spot for three weeks. The liquid is then strained off and served as a drink of delightful quality and strength. The wood of the Krania is a hardwood, so resilient that the branches were used as spokes in wheels and it is ideal for the shepherds' glitsas. The curved crook itself is usually made of hand carved wood or bone, even horn.

Years ago, from an antique shop in Sussex, I had bought a Victorian Bo-Peep type crook made of iron with a graceful, sinuous curve and I took it down to the plateia for inspection. It was handed from one to another, viewed from all angles and tested to prove its authenticity by sliding the thickest part of the thumb up the shaft and into the crook. As long as the thumb didn't get stuck it was deemed the genuine article, a male thumb being equivalent in thickness to a lamb's ankle so that if the shepherd needs to capture or rescue a lamb he knows he can successfully hook him round the leg and pull him in. My Victorian crook passed muster.

As the evenings became cooler, the trucks began to turn up and within a week the shepherds had migrated back to the lowlands. The kafeneon stayed open for a few days more then closed its doors until spring. The village and its fifteen inhabitants settled down for the winter, and a strong sense of unity and village identity prevailed, instinctive perhaps but vital for the survival of a small mountain community. Although this would be our first winter in such comparative isolation we had a comfortable feeling that we would be well looked after.

The word Koukouli is Greek for 'cocoon' and in days gone by the women of the village bred silk worms. We learned all this from the spinster sisters, Thalia and Aspasia, whose mother, widowed at an early age with two daughters to raise, turned to the silkworm for her income and built up a small cottage industry. She made her living from sewing and embroidering garments for the wealthy ladies in Ioannina, and weaving and looming wool into rugs and flokatis. Thalia and Aspasia, now both in their seventies and lively as crickets, proudly showed us some of her work. Exquisitely complicated floral designs in glowing colours on the hem of a black silk apron, traditionally worn by the women of Zagoria; a 'sagouni', a sleeveless jacket reaching below the knee, in soft black felt, a fabric they made themselves, and heavily embroidered in scarlet silk all around the edges and partway down the back. The designs are knotted and whorled, ribbed and raised, and an elaborately embroidered jacket was a sign of wealth. Again, the sagouni was worn by the women, and the sisters pressed Effie into putting it on and wearing it a while. Not a dedicated follower of fashion, even I could see what a stunning garment it was, utterly dateless with its simplicity of cut, and the colours as radiant as the day it was made.

Thalia, noting our enthusiasm, produced from an inlaid domed chest a waistcoat that had taken her mother six years to embroider. These beautiful things, smelling faintly of mothballs, were the few remaining items left of their mother's work. After her death most had been sold, when times were hard and ready money needed, to dealers who probably paid a pittance, and have disappeared forever.

"The Girls" as the two are fondly called, live just over the wall from us and by the wall, in our garden, stands a big, old, white mulberry tree. Doubtless their mother would have used the leaves to feed her precious silkworms. With age and heavy pollarding it had grown into a black, moss covered, mangled shape and both Effie and Papa Kostas were agreed that it should be cut down. Effie's viewpoint was that the tree was ugly and most likely diseased, Papa Kostas' that in summer when fruiting it would be swarming with bees and hornets. Being of a slightly sentimental nature I wasn't buying either argument. The tree was far older than me - far older than the house - and it had historic associations. If the summer swarming proved to be a hazard then we could review its fate. In retrospect I have a feeling that Papa Kostas was more interested in it as a source of logs for winter than as a tree. During the following summer we never saw a single wasp, bee, hornet or even fly near it. Instead it was filled with a cheerful chattering flock of birds, openly stealing the fruit. The tree stayed.

Koukouli is a relatively small village and lies in a natural, crescent shaped hollow in the hills, a thousand metres above sea level, surrounded by uninterrupted woodland and facing south, catching the sun from dawn to dusk. Twisting cobbled lanes link the houses, some of which are being gradually restored, whilst others, beyond the expense to do so, are sadly decaying and falling down. Yet others which have completely caved in have been cleared of stone and turned into vegetable plots instead, the outer walls and lychgates conveniently keeping out stray goats and sheep. Violets, red dead nettle, blue bugle, cranesbill and comfrey grow out of the walls and between the cobbles, and ivy, bramble, wild rose and old man's beard cover the shapeless mounds of uncleared masonry.

Strangely enough, the church, instead of being central to the village, is the final building to the east. The settlement of Koukouli developed after a shepherd, led by the flocks, discovered the 'springs' some time before the fourteenth century. The inhabitants of three ancient settlements in the area moved to the site and began building their houses below the springs round the curve of the hill westwards. A church, a small one, was built on the site of those first springs. From 1400 - 1650 the village prospered and grew, and during that time the larger church was built and in 1630 enlarged. Later, between 1750 and 1860 Koukouli enjoyed a second phase of prosperity and in 1796 the church was again enlarged. The menfolk who had travelled abroad to work, principally to Eastern European countries, returned wealthy and built mansions for their families, often influenced by the style of houses they had seen on their travels. They gave money, or set up trusts and bequests to finance the local council, and it was this wealth that funded the building of the school and well arches. It also paid for a hospice, where a room and food could be obtained by any traveller arriving in the village. No charge was made for this hospitality, but it was expected that the hospice caretaker should be recompensed suitably for his services. The community funds also bought school books, incense for the church, paid for a resident Papas and school teacher and a village beadle, whose job it was to patrol the village and its lands. On March 13th, 1813, the plane tree was planted in the village square, a date firmly remembered by the villagers even now. There was a butcher, a shoemaker and general store to serve a resident population of over four hundred Koukouliotises.

This then was the answer as to how these villages

had prospered well enough to build so grandly and endow large schools, churches and public buildings in an area so remote, offering little in natural resources save water and stone. In addition, during the 18th and much of the 19th centuries, when Greece was under Turkish domination, many Zagorians held high positions in Constantinople, and for this reason, and by virtue of their remoteness, the villages enjoyed certain privileges. In the time of Ali Pasha's rule in Ioannina, from 1788 to 1822, they were given the right to administer their affairs autonomously in return for the regular and prompt payment of taxes. Koukouli no doubt benefitted from being the home village of Manthos Oikonomou, economic adviser to Ali Pasha and a close colleague. But with the death of Ali these privileges were gradually revoked and from 1868 Zagoria suffered a long and unremitting period of banditry.

The church, however, remained unscathed, and is still the religious and social centre of the life of the village. It is recognised as being one of the most beautifully decorated churches in all Zagoria, with a high carved and gilded lectern, and vast crystal chandeliers brought over from Russia and donated to the church. Upon entering through a low, triple arched doorway of carved stone you find yourself in the narthex, a walled area with windows and doors screened with wooden lattice work from whence women and strangers could follow the service since they were not allowed into the actual church. On our first visit, being cautious, we stayed in the narthex, but soon spotted were ushered through into the nave and I shall never forget the sheer awesomeness of entering into that wonderful vaulted edifice. Not one inch of wall space was left unpainted to tell the story of the Gospel and the lives of the saints. On a background of deepest gentian, the brilliant colours of the saints' robes and the flickering gold of their haloes caught by the candlelight and light from the heavy hanging chandeliers, filled the church with a sense of infinite richness and boundless mystery. The high, intricately carved and exquisitely gilded screen, or iconostasis, separating the nave from the sanctuary, is richly hung with icons, and the radiance reflected from it draws the eye and concentrates the mind. Robed in gold, Papa Kostas conducts the service from the sanctuary and in front of the iconostasis, his chanting voice mingling with the smoke and incense rising through the air. Above the centre of the iconostasis a fabulously embossed cross is illuminated by beams of light from a small window behind it in the eastern wall of the apse, radiating all around it. If your eyes follow the smoke even higher, you can see, painted on the ceiling of the dome way above, the image of Pantokrator the Almighty, sternly regarding everyone from aloft.

Papa Kostas and his family are the youngest people in the village and we, second youngest. This statistical achievement is not difficult to comprehend when you realise that the average age of the rest of the village residents is over seventy! Papa Kostas and Elevtheria originate from villages a good way south of Ioannina where he had been apprenticed to the building trade. He became ordained as a priest when he was twenty four, and the church offered him a posting in the neighbouring village of Kipi. However there was no house available which meant he would be obliged to travel from his distant home village, not an entirely satisfactory arrangement either for the Papas with three young babies or the congregation of Kipi.

At the same time Koukouli was without a priest and Petros and Maria, then with two growing children and anxious to bring other young life into the community, managed to find accommodation that Papa Kostas could rent for a nominal fee and so, he became instead the Papas for Koukouli. To our surprise we discovered that the house they'd been renting in those early days had been ours; they had lived in the larger of the two for several years and young Georgos, their fourth child, had actually been born there. Sometimes they still refer to it as 'our old house'.

Village priests in Greece are expected and encouraged to have another job to supplement their income, and Papa Kostas soon found building work in Koukouli and neighbouring villages. He bought a piece of land within the village and over the years built his own house in traditional style, an excellent advertisement for his skills, hard work and resourcefulness.

For several months after we arrived he had been working restoring a big house higher up in the village and I used to wander up towards evening to see how he was getting on. We were standing on the roof, which he was stripping, marvelling at the spectacular view from that vantage point when he asked me about my religion. I had to confess to not being of any religious bent. I explained that this probably stemmed from schooldays when we were forced to attend church regularly and listen to some pious parson harping on about the rewards for keeping to the straight and narrow when we all knew he was having it off with the local postmistress. At this, Papa Kostas roared with laughter and from behind a pile of stones produced a little bottle of chipero and up there, in the evening light, we drank to crazy English prelates.

The following Sunday, in an attempt to support our local priest, we decided to go to church. The services are over two hours long and in the winter, apart from Petros and Khristogolou who chant the responses, most people just turn up for the last half hour. Standing at the back it occurred to me how soulless it must be for a priest in a village such as ours with so sparse a congregation. Yet there was Papa Kostas in full swing, chanting sincerely and devoutly in his strong, resonant voice, giving the service every ounce of his concentration just as though the church had been packed. Everything he did, it seemed, he did wholeheartedly and to the maximum of his capabilities. As a Papas in the church he was impressive, moving and credible. But I still couldn't help myself staring at him in semi-disbelief. Was this really the same man I had been sharing a drink with on a roof top only the other day?

Later that afternoon, in grubby working jeans and a plaster covered pullover, he came up to borrow a spade and asked what we thought of the service. It was very impressive, we told him, despite the fact we couldn't understand a single word.

"Oh, don't worry about that - neither does anyone else, much. It's all in Ancient Greek," he said, and breezed off.

I could see that Papa Kostas was not terribly interested in whether we were Catholic or Protestant; he was not a sanctimonious zealot and had no intention of forcing Greek Orthodoxy down our throats. He was quite simply a cheerful, hard working, family man who genuinely believed in his God conscientiously and humanely. From time to time we go to church and share in the various religious celebrations and Saints' Days, and there seem to be no pressures put on anyone that we can see. The services are conducted to a relaxed gathering of people who have joined together in a sincere and unaffected belief and faith. I admire them for it being such a part of their lives and daily conduct, and I admire the sense of continuity. A far cry from my schooldays.

Some years ago, Papa Kostas had got his hands on two plots of land not far from his house, to grow vegetables. With six mouths to feed, a sound investment. On one plot he has put in three walnut trees, and plants it out with potatoes and onions. His other plot was on a steep hillside below the bell tower and needed a large retaining wall before it could be cultivated. With the help of a couple of itinerant Albanians the wall was built, but after the first heavy rains half of it promptly gave way and the stones rolled far down the hillside ending up in a stream at the bottom. I surveyed the mess, knowing how disappointed I would be if the wall had been mine, and sympathised with him. He shrugged, lit a cigarette, said there was plenty of stone about and, this time without the Albanians, doggedly started the whole slow building process again. It's a lovely garden now, planted out with forty vines in neat rows at one end and, in season, tomatoes, lettuce, spinach and garlic at the other.

Almost everybody has a plot or plots of land. Maria and Petros have several, and Thalia and Aspasia have two or more which they till, plant and harvest entirely on their own. Once the stones have been picked out, a matter of twenty years labour it would seem, and assisted by the regular and generous application of goat shit, the supply being plentiful, the earth is rich, dark and fertile. The self-sufficiency craze died in England years ago, looked upon as eccentric and the butt of many jokes, later to revive itself on more commercial lines in the form of Organic Farming. Here it has never been a fad. It started when the village first formed and was and still is a way of life. Thalia and Aspasia had taken us to see their enormous basements down in the depths of their house. Laid out, rack upon rack, were their winter stocks of potatoes, onions, apples, quince, garlic, maize and walnuts. In another dark corner were the barrels of wine that Papa Kostas makes for them and, of course, chipero. There were tins of feta cheese, and galotiri, a creamed cheese, literally milk-cheese. In these cavernous cellars the temperature never varies winter or summer and to see, stored there all the work and produce of the two seventy year old sisters made us feel more than a little inadequate. At this time of the year though, the plots lay at rest, carefully tilled and mulched, until the first days of spring sunshine awaken them to provide again.

Mr. Biffet was still happily lounging in the lap of luxury on Corfu and we had no regrets for not having brought him to Koukouli to wreak his special brand of destruction on an otherwise passive village. All our married life we had had a dog or two and it felt strange at first not to have the routine that any canine will insist you perform daily for its well being. It came as a surprise to us to find in Koukouli four happy, good natured, well fed dogs, particularly as the Greeks are not generally renowned for their love of domestic animals. An even greater surprise was to find that none of these dogs had Greek names. Papa Kostas' dog, a total wimp and coward, was called 'Boomer'. 'Jaques', whose direct ancestor must have modelled for His Master's Voice, belonged to Khristogolou at the other end of the village. 'Booky', belonging to Petros and Maria, was a handsome rusty coloured dog with amber eyes who took three months to stop rushing out to attack us. The breakthrough with him came on our return from a brief visit to England. He vaulted the wall, threw two immense muddy paws round my neck and tried to kiss me to death.

Since this remarkable change of heart he has been the most companionable of dogs and a trusted neighbour. The only female dog in the village belongs to Thalia and Aspasia. An enormous black and tan tart of a girl, Lucy has become the village bicycle and produces endless litters of allsorts with no proud father claiming custodial rights.

None of the dogs are tied up, they freely roam the village, sleeping in their owners' outhouses at night. The puzzle to us was why they had dogs at all? Cats, insular as they are, do at least catch vermin, but a dog? The answer came when, one night, a terrific clatter of dogs passed our bedroom windows, pounding in unison down the lane and setting up a chorus of continual barking for the next hour. In the morning Papa Kostas told us that the previous day a vagrant Albanian had been spotted, camping out rough in the woodlands. That night he had tried to steal into the village but our gang had seen him off. They also guard the village from the intrusion of foxes and on rare occasions, wolves, that might threaten their livestock. None of the dogs themselves touch or even seem to notice the chicken, sheep or goats, but we did chance to catch Lucy one day, up to no good. Elevtheria had let her chicken out but left the coop door open. Lucy coolly tip-toed into the hen hut and reappeared with an egg delicately held in her mouth. Round the corner and out of sight, she gently put the egg on the ground, nipped the shell with her front teeth until a hole was made, and lapped up the contents. Not a drop was lost, all that remained was the tell-tale shell. With this motley crew we found we had the company of dogs without the hassle and responsibility of ownership. We made it a rule never to feed them or in anyway encourage them to make their homes with us, but weakened enough to give them a drop of milk when they came calling.

A big house next to the village square, with walls fortified like a castle, belongs to a friendly and charming man called Michalis and his equally friendly wife, Fo-fo. They spend most of their summer here and the rest of the year in their flat on Corfu. Michalis is a retired policeman and, having worked with the Tourist Police, speaks a good smattering of English. His father had inherited three properties in Koukouli. One was now a complete ruin which he and Fo-fo have cleared and made into a sizeable vegetable garden, the second was their large house by the square and the third had been our property. We had found the link! It had been Michalis' father who had sold our property to Mr. Ferandinos, and he confirmed that our titles to it were, indeed, squeaky clean.

There are, scattered around the mountains, perched in high and seemingly inaccessible places, tiny churches with large open porches big enough to shelter travellers on horseback with their retinue. Agios Minas is one of these and Michalis told us that since the next day was Saint Minas' Day there would be a service in the church. People from Koukouli would go up and others from the village of Kapesovo, equidistant from the church, would come down and if we wanted to go, he would show us how to get there.

Through lashing rain and eddies of leaves we followed him up the track behind the village, climbing and looping uphill, the mist swirling around us, clouds suddenly releasing a view of distant mountain and as suddenly blotting it out. A camera shutter of views, snapped and lost again. The wind tore through and the cold was bitter. There must have been over thirty people assembled when we arrived and the tiny church could barely hold twenty. Papa

Kostas was delivering the service and had already been underway for an hour and a half. Standing outside in the open porch, images of bowls of hot soup hovered, only to be swept away by another high-speed cloud. It became routine to take it in turns to squeeze into the little doorway and have a quick warm-up by the floor standing candelabrum, stuffed with an astonishing amount of candles, before squeezing out again to make way for another frozen parishioner.

Fo-fo had wisely opted out of this arctic experience and on our return welcomed us with hot coffee, several chiperos and a blazing fire. Papa Kostas had often complained about how cold his feet got, standing long hours on cold, damp flagstones and now we knew just what he meant. Effie came to his rescue by giving him a pair of her thick, thermal, mountaineering socks. The colour wasn't quite the thing for a Papas but under the long cassock not much noticed, and they were worn most Sundays during wintertime.

By now, our bathroom was finished, panelled in an Edwardian fashion with oil-lamp style wall lights and wooden fittings. The kitchen was next on our list. The new fridge freezer was installed and we had bought a large cooker with four gas and two electric hobs, and an oven with grill and spit mechanism large enough to take half a lamb, the perfect cooker for when the hotel was up and running. The worktops we'd decided were to be of solid, two inch thick pine, untreated and, like butchers' blocks, easily scrubbed and kept clean. I would make wall cupboards incorporating a Turkish motif and under- counter cupboards to match, bringing a certain Zagorian flavour to the thing. With a little juggling and, as it turned out, near miraculous joinery, the washing machine could be hidden away behind matching doors. The kitchen door itself was to have a window in it at head height, to avoid accidents to-ing and fro-ing, echoing the shape on the cupboards. While I was working on this, knee deep in sawdust, screws and spirit levels, Effie was putting a gooey sealant onto the rough plastered walls to stop them flaking and give a good base for paint. We had grown just a bit tired of cement grey as an overall theme, and it would be wonderful to clear away a few boxes and get more organised.

The trees had shed their leaves and revealed themselves covered with thick lichen, hanging from the branches like delicate lacework, a pale, luminescent green that became spectacularly fresh after a fall of rain, sparkling with captured droplets. Only the oak held onto their last shreds of leaves, glowing burnished and brown amongst the other trees. Wind, storm and rain failed to dislodge them and they would hang on until the new buds bursting finally pushed them off the trees in spring.

Chipero and Christmas

The villages in Zagoria grow their own vines but not enough to make wine in any quantity. However, in October, the grape lorries come up from the Peloponnese and tour Northern Greece. The arrival of the lorry is announced by a loudspeaker on the roof of the cab blaring dreadful tinny music whilst the driver, in a gravelly, slurred voice-over, advertises his wares. He parks in front of the church and lets down the tailgate. Brightly coloured plastic crates, blue, red, green, yellow are stacked high inside, full of grapes to be sold by the pallet load.

Papa Kostas and Elevtheria, Petros and Maria, Thalia and the taller Aspasia, head held characteristically on one side, gather round, together with Khristogolou, Marigoula and Manolis from the other end of the village. Crates are handed down and examined, rejected, haggled over, until all their various caches are selected and separately stacked. Meanwhile the music blares on and the driver's wife lolls in the cab with a couple of children peering through the windscreen from behind a pelmet of pointed crochet hung with medallions, crucifixes, worry beads and a string of flashing Christmas tree lights. Eventually, money exchanging hands, the driver hauls himself into the cab, slams the door, switches off the music and roars slowly away down the track. Everyone is left to compare their purchases, discuss the deal, bemoan the increased prices since last year and make arrangements for getting their crates home.

Thalia and Aspasia are demons at making hooch. It was at their house we had our first taste of Kranol, made from the berries of the Krania, a dark port-coloured drink, served to us in exquisite and very old sherry glasses. They smiled encouragingly, we smiled back and I took my first sip. As the liquid slid slowly down it was soft and gentle with an unusual but very pleasing, non-sweet flavour. I smiled again, and then... POW! It hit all my internal tubes like liquid X-ray!

Asked whether I liked it I managed to splutter, in a falsetto voice through disappearing breath and watering eyes, that it was very pleasant indeed. With their own grapes from a vine that completely covers their garden pergola, they make about twenty bottles of an excellent, sparkling, rosé which is lovingly stored in their cool cellars and not touched for at least eight years, and then only on very special occasions.

After the arrival of the grape lorries, the frenzied cleaning and scrubbing of barrels can be heard from courtyards and outhouses, spouts flow and the streets run with water. 'The Girls' still use great, old, wooden casks, but Papa Kostas makes his wine in huge modern plastic barrels. The end product is drunk as soon as it has fermented. Experience of this too-young, proudly offered wine has led us to avoid it like the plague. It's a foul tasting, murky pink, pond-water concoction. But to be offered a glass some six months later is another matter - it has developed into a clear, light rosé, kind to the palate and very drinkable. To be honest, the Greeks, though the first to produce wine, have never really progressed in the field of viniculture and to compare a locally made Greek wine with any other would be sheer lunacy. Their only valid claim is that their wine is 'horis pharmaco' – without the chemicals used in commercial production.

Once the winemaking is out of the way, there comes the serious business of chipero making. Papa Kostas drives to his father's village and returns with the still, a much used, Heath Robinson contraption which has to be set up in his outhouse and takes several hours to assemble. Sensing my obvious curiosity, he asked if I would like to lend him a hand, although he already had his three sons eagerly helping. First of all a large trivet is put in place on the stone floor and levelled. Onto this goes a blackened witches' cauldron with two handles. On top of the cauldron sits a great bell shaped lid. A copper pipe rises vertically from the apex of this lid for about two feet then turns at right angles and runs along at a slight slope for six or seven feet, before bending again and disappearing down into an oil-drum. Inside the drum it links to a centre column of copper tubing forming a coil which connects to a small brass tap about a foot above the bottom of the drum.

With this all assembled, well pleased with our efforts and bolstered by several preliminary chiperos to set the mood, we started with the actual distilling. A huge fire of logs and old planks was built under the trivet. The oil drum was filled to the brim with cold water. There was one hosepipe to keep it topped up and another to drain water off in order to keep it constantly cool for the distillation process. Papa Kostas lined the cauldron with fresh dry straw and filled it up with must from the previous winemaking - all the pips, bits of leaves and twigs, with some unfermented grape juice added. With the cauldron settled on the trivet over the fire, the bell was carefully lowered into position and the joins thoroughly sealed with a paste composed of wood ash and flour. Finally a pan was put on the floor under the tap in the oil drum and covered with a clean muslin napkin to protect the ensuing contents from flying wood ash. Everything was ready, but it would be an hour before there were any results and the fire had to be tended all the time to keep the heat output constant.

Darkness fell and there were now fourteen people sitting round the cauldron, sipping the remains of last year's chipero. Food was brought, bread was toasted on the embers, and chestnuts split and roasted. A contented dog lay with his back to the fire, feet outstretched. There was a mediaeval quality to the scene and sitting in that dark outhouse with the heavy smoke filtering through blackened beams, faces lit by flickering firelight, I had the strangest sensation of being in an oil painting, an Old Master that I'd seen somewhere before, but was unable to name. Suddenly a loud cheer went up as the first few drops plonked into the saucepan from the tap. Half an hour would produce one litre and by the end of two hours the must in the cauldron would need to be replaced. The first drops turned to a steady trickle and as soon as there was enough in the pan, Papa Kostas checked it with an alcoholometer. Then he dipped a glass in and took a taste, held it up to the light and scrutinised the contents, took another sip and passed the glass round for a consensus of opinion. They agreed it was high on alcohol but this apparently was expected with the first batch and now the still was fully warmed up, the second should be perfect.

Changeover came, the bell was hit with a lump of wood to break the seal and, with the aid of damp cloths, lowered to the ground. The steaming cauldron was lifted away on two poles and the contents emptied into a corner. This residual mulch would be dug into the kitchen garden later. Scoured, refilled and back on the trivet with the bell replaced and sealed, it was only a matter of twenty minutes before the chipero started to trickle again.

At two in the morning, Papa Kostas and I, considerably the worse for wear, were the last to leave. We checked that the fire was safe and, with arms round each other for stability, staggered the few yards to his house. A final, unwanted chipero was thrust into my hand after which I zigzagged my way home. Undeservedly, I awoke the next morning without the slightest trace of a hangover and looking from the upstairs window could see the smoke seeping through Papa Kostas' outhouse roof. He had already started production and would continue the pattern for the next few days.

Chipero is made in every village throughout Zagoria at this time of the year and my thorough and exhaustive one-man survey confirms that there are as many variants as with malt whiskies. Some are tangy, some smooth, some smoky, some sharp and some undrinkable. Basically it's a pure, clear drink about 40% proof and has been aptly described as a 'rustic spirit of potency and charm'. In Mikro Papingo, the chipero is particularly smooth, and we were amused to discover that it is made there in a little annex which is an integral part of the church! A happy and successful union between God and the devil.

After Papa Kostas had finished with the still it was dismantled and set up in the outhouse of Petros and Maria. One evening, having just finished supper, a blast from the tannoy let it be known that we were wanted at their house. Sensing some urgency we scampered over the wall into their yard only to find that we had been inveigled into another chipero-making session. Their outbuilding was very much smaller than Papa Kostas' but had narrow banquettes around the walls covered in thick, home spun flokatis. A table between was laden with bottles and food. I lay back on the banquette, Pasha style, with Effie beside me. The heat from the fire in so enclosed an area was tremendous and the smoke hung low against the rafters; so low that when anyone stood up you were suddenly confronted with a headless coughing torso.

Petros, who had been fussing around the still, poking at the fire, and adding wood, had the nervous habit of wiping his face with his hands and, as the evening wore on his hands and consequently his face became blacker and blacker. Effie, aided and abetted by Maria's constant topping up of glasses, was becoming decidedly giggly. Looking up at Petros she suddenly pointed at him, shrieked "Othello!" and sank back onto the flokati in uncontrollable mirth. I'm quite sure the subtlety of her joke was lost on the rest of the party but the more she laughed the more they laughed, until the whole group was reduced to hysterics. Petros' face by now was black as night with just the whites of his eyes penetrating the smoke from beneath his baseball cap. Without warning and quite unexpectedly he took it upon himself to play the part of a bedouin, hands together, bowing and salaaming for all he was worth. It was just too funny for words and once again the party was on the floor with laughter. Any passer by, seeing us at that moment in a smoke filled shed on a cold November night, would have had us all arrested and certified.

Weak with exhaustion and countless chiperos, Effie struggled to her feet and with a large, mechanical wave bid everyone goodnight. She stumbled out through the low door followed by a dramatic pall of smoke. Two seconds later a loud crash and the sound of tin cans rattling over cobbles, followed by an outburst of strangulated giggles, warned us that her progress was going to be slow and potentially dangerous. Maria went to her rescue and gently led her home and helped her to bed. I left the party some time later, carefully avoiding the wreckage my wife had strewn in her wake. I found her in bed, fully clothed beneath the duvet, a wonderful smile on her face. She was fast asleep.

Khristogolou and Pepitsa, the owners of Jaques, live at the other side of the village. Khristo is a retired schoolteacher, a slightly arthritic man in his late sixties, of teddy bear proportions. His natural conversational tone is that of a sergeant major, and because we are foreigners he has hit upon the idea of shouting at us in a mixture of four languages, excluding English. This kindly-meant, international gesture has us nodding intelligently without having the slightest idea of what he has said. Only after unscrambling some of the less important words can we come close to guessing what it could be.

As a result of one of these deciphered conversations I found myself driving Suzi up the mountainside to some distant village with Khristo, smartly dressed in jacket and tie and sporting his winter hat, a variant on a 1930's flying helmet, sitting beside me. I soon came to realise that every time he adjusted his hat a new set of directions would follow. The fact that I knew where we were going in no way deterred him. The purpose of our mission, as I understood it, was to purchase some cheese. It did strike me that this was a long way to go to buy cheese, particularly as I knew he had been to Ioannina on the bus only the day before. He jabbed the windscreen excitedly as we caught sight of our destination. I parked in the square and followed him up lanes and round corners arriving at a house on the outskirts of the village.

Settled in the kitchen with a roaring stove, it came as a relief to me to see that even these people appeared to be struggling to understand him. This observation seemed borne out when a notepad and pen were brought to the table, but I was mistaken. Khristo was negotiating the price of the cheese. Grim looks were exchanged, more scribbles made, chipero was brought out as a pause factor and, after further scribblings on a diminishing notepad, smiles all round as a price was agreed. Thank heavens for that. We all trooped into the yard and from a shed a massive twenty-five kilo tin of feta was carried out. Now this was serious cheese buying. Even more serious were the other four, twenty-five kilo tins that followed it!

'What the dickens is he going to do with it all?' I thought. 'There's only him and Pepitsa.'

The lids were prised open and the contents inspected and tasted. I went back to bring the car as near as possible to the house and the cheesemaker's wife and I lugged the monster cans into the back - Khristo was too busy counting out drachmas onto the kitchen table.

On the way home I couldn't resist asking him, "You and Pepitsa eat a lot of feta, do you?"

"Not so very much, no."

"Well then, what are we doing with a hundred and twenty five kilos of the stuff in the back of the car?"

"Oh that," he replied, looking over his shoulder to verify there was any there at all. "Good heavens, it's not just for us. No, no, we couldn't possibly eat all that! Most of it's for my sons in Germany - they're mad about feta!" And he roared with laughter.

My thoughts turned idly to the idea of Khristo attempting to post twenty-five kilo tins of feta to Germany, but I deemed it best not to ask any more questions.

Some weeks after Christmas he turned up again, excitable as ever, asking when we next planned to go to Ioannina as his television had broken down and he needed to get it to the service man. Two days later, outside his house, we were struggling with a giant, vintage, twenty-six inch television with an enormous bump behind, housing the tube. With her hood on, Suzi doesn't have unlimited space in the back, and it took several permutations to get the television safely installed, leaving a tiny gap for Khristo. I suggested that it would be far better to let Effie sit in the back as she was so much smaller, but no - he wouldn't hear of it. With help from Pepitsa, who clearly found the whole escapade vastly amusing, we eased him into position around the television and he resolutely replaced his hat which had come off in the fray.

Partway to Ioannina I could see in the rear view mirror that Khristo was seriously suffering from being so cramped. I stopped the car and after some argument, pride on his part dictating over discomfort, I managed to persuade him to change places with Effie by saying I would need him in the front in Ioannina, for directions to find the service centre.

Once there, we turned off the main street into a complex of side streets, and I could tell by his frantic hat adjustments that we had become hopelessly lost.

"Ah ha! Up here... left here... now down! This is right. This is right!"

Which brought us back to where we had started. Repeating this manoeuvre twice, but from different directions, I suggested we ask one of the men at a cafe whose faces, by now, were becoming familiar. This proved a wise move as we quickly learned that the service centre was just round the corner from the cafe. Manhandling the television into the shop, I saw the service man's face drop when he caught sight of Khristo's beaming smile accompanied by vociferous explanations. Gloriously, it was impossible for him to repair the set in under two weeks, which dissolved my mounting fears for the return journey to Koukouli with the television, our shopping, Khristo, and all his shopping!

We had had a phone call from Jo and Vasilis, Mr. Biffet's new owners. Could we possibly find a cottage for them and their two small children to rent for a couple of weeks over the Christmas holidays? This year Vasilis was putting his foot down and was refusing to suffer another Christmas on Corfu with its endless stream of obligatory parties given by the growing English community for their children. We suggested that a cottage in Kipi, belonging to Eleni our architect, would be ideal, and went on to describe it.

"Sounds wonderful! Could you arrange everything for us?"

Politely I declined and gave him instead Eleni's phone number to contact her himself. Effie and I had long ago given up making holiday arrangements for anybody, however close they may be as friends. Countless times on Corfu we booked car hire, hotels, apartments, only to be met with:-

"Oh, we didn't expect to have to pay quite so much!"

"Not what we wanted at all, sorry!"

"Couldn't you have found us something a bit bigger?"

"This won't do for us old chap! Have to find somewhere nearer the sea."

Vasilis was not in the least put out, however. He runs his own travel agency and understands the business well enough to appreciate our point of view. A few days later he rang again to say that he had booked the cottage, letting us know their date of arrival. He planned to come up to Koukouli first to collect the keys which Eleni was to leave with us.

Living in England, I had come over the years to actively loathe Christmas. Once Guy Fawkes Night has passed the build-up starts with a vengeance: newscasters with a sparkling tree behind them, gaudy decorations everywhere, increased traffic, artificial jolliness, Jingle Bells, and horrendous office parties. The hype grows as Christmas Day approaches. Arrangements are made with relatives, who can't stand the sight of each other, to get together. Sighs of relief when that cantankerous old so-and-so, Aunt Flo, says she can't make it.

"Never mind, dear. Next year maybe?"
Food, enough to mount a siege, is brought home by the boot-load, including the obligatory boxes of dates nobody eats. Drink by the caseload is bought for friends and neighbours who flock in droves to drink it, led by that miserable blighter from across the way who wouldn't even lend you a screwdriver when asked. Plastic toys are broken within minutes amid howls of tears, or come supplied without batteries so more tears. The total sincerity of a "Happy Christmas" dies on the day with fractious children, and a family row waged between aging aunts and well oiled uncles in paper hats.

Only in recent years have the Greeks begun to celebrate Christmas in any noticeable way. Not because it holds any great importance in their religious calendar, but there are, admittedly, some commercial opportunities to be gained. Even so, it's a very low key affair, which doesn't get under way until two weeks before Christmas Day. Some modest decorations appear in shop windows and the local municipality hangs lights through the streets in Ioannina, more really in readiness for their more important New Year celebrations. Street vendors start selling dreadful Father Christmases and blow-up reindeer along with plastic trees and tinsel. But apart from this, if you live in a village like Koukouli, Christmas could come and go without anyone noticing. I love Christmas here without all the commercialism. We have a normal, unhassled shopping session in Ioannina with a few Christmas additives. Simple presents, bought or hand made, are given as tokens of friendship rather than to impress, and people wish each other "Kalo Khristouyenna", "Happy Christmas", and they mean it.

Real Christmas trees can be bought in town, at inflated prices, but it has always seemed to us, long before the Green Movement, a pointless exercise decorating a dying tree in your living room. One November day we had taken a drive with friends to the village of Vradhetto, north of Koukouli and the highest village in Zagoria. After coffees in the square, we took a walk out to 'Beloi', a vantage point right on the cliff top overlooking the Vikos Gorge. Probably the most spectacular view in Europe unfolds, down to the depths of the Gorge, and the eye follows its winding course to where the mountains of Greece and Albania intertwine and soar. On the way back, Effie spotted an enormous candelabra thistle standing a full seven feet tall, its dead heads hanging down like crystals on a chandelier. It was a perfect shape, with branches radiating out in widening symmetry from the single, upright stem.

"That," she cried, delightedly, "will be our Christmas Tree!"

Orders given, I tugged and pulled and triumphantly carried this prickly object back to the car. There was considerable difficulty easing the thing in without breaking or damaging it, but with the top half sticking out through the passenger window we got it home, and hung it up, temporarily, in the old building. Papa Kostas' children came round to see it and were totally unimpressed.

"This? Your Christmas Tree?" exclaimed Kiki. "How?"

Prepared for this, Effie produced four cans of coloured aerosol paints. Giving one to each of the children she directed them in turn where to spray. The main body of the plant was dark green, but the pendulous heads, like baubles, were sprayed red, gold and silver, using newspaper to mask the rest of the plant. As it developed the children began to be much more enthusiastic, offering the idea of lightly over-spraying the green with silver to give it a frosted effect. Two hours of concentrated effort, and a very different thistle stood before them, and we all agreed that the very best place for it would be to hang it from a ceiling beam over the stairwell in the living room. Young Georgos stayed behind and helped me struggle to get it in position, fussing about where I should bang in the nail, and departed well pleased with the end result.

Effie had begun Christmas preparations by making a massive bowl of mincemeat. To my untrained eye in these matters it seemed a huge amount for two people. Gentle questioning revealed that she planned to make two hundred mince pies – some to offer to visitors, and some to be given to the villagers.

"But what if they don't like them? You know how conservative the Greeks are with food. If it isn't something their grandmothers used to make..."

"Then you'll have to eat them."

Eating two hundred mince pies was not the way I had planned my entry into The Guinness Book of Records, and I hoped beyond all hope that the villagers would like them. I consoled myself with the thought that the village dogs could surreptitiously be persuaded to help out if it came to the bottom line.

Our experiences on Corfu with fresh turkey had not been good. The trouble with the Greek butchers' fresh turkey is that they never hang them. Fresh means FRESH: killed, plucked and into the oven in just the same manner as their chicken come out of the yard and into the pot. But in Ioannina we found a section of the supermarket freezing cabinet suddenly turned over to frozen, all-American turkey, with built in Auto-Pop-Up-Timer! The fascination for me lay more with the Pop-Up-Timer than the actual turkey, but it couldn't be worse than our previous efforts so we bought one. Effie made a traditional English stuffing, spending hours fiddling about with chestnuts which we'd been given by the bushel. We were beginning to get nicely into a Christmassy mood and the discovery of a bottle of Port in a small wine shop in town, to go with the Stilton some kind person had mailed us from England, set the seal.

Jo and Vasilis arrived a few days before Christmas, with a trailer to carry all the toys, foodstuffs, clothes and general paraphernalia that two small children seem to require. They had brought us three litres of olive oil, pressed from their own olives, but when we went to the car

110

to go with them to Kipi, the trailer seemed to be suffering from slight incontinence. A steady trickle of oil was dribbling from the back corner. Vasilis rushed to open the trailer lid and there, in a wicker basket in the corner, stood the olive oil. The two glass bottles had survived the journey, but the plastic bottle had split, presumably made brittle by the cold.

"Who was the FOOL who packed this?" he cried. "A three year old could have done better!"

"You did," Jo calmly replied, swatting the kids out of habit before they giggled. Fortunately, parked on a slight incline, the oil had drained straight out of the trailer and nothing was seriously damaged. We helped them unpack in Kipi and carry everything up to the cottage, lit the stove, switched on the immersion heater and left them to settle in.

That evening, we took some of the remaining oil down to Papa Kostas and his family. They were all upstairs in their living room. He and Elevtheria had put a small trivet over the hot ashes in the fireplace and on it was a thin, flat stone. When the stone was hot enough, they rubbed wood ash over it and poured three tablespoons of batter onto it. The batter bubbled and baked, making three thin slices of excellent pitta bread, with a faint woody taste from the ash which effectively prevented the batter sticking to the stone. The slices were handed round as they were baked, and we all ate them with fried feta cheese and pickled onions, a custom originating from their home village, and observed once a year on the night before Christmas Eve.

On Christmas Eve itself, Jo and Vasilis and the children came round for supper. They were over the moon with the cottage and the children were having the time of their lives. What surprised everyone was how well they kept themselves amused without the aid of television or video or the usual stimulus of people and other children constantly dropping in.

Afterwards, we trooped all together to the late church service. Papa Kostas was resplendent in his robes beyond the golden iconostasis which gleamed with the reflection of the lights and candles, against the darkness all around. The children's eyes were wide, black pools in their little upturned faces as they gazed at it all in wonderment. The church, however, was freezingly cold. Petros had lit an insignificant wood-burning stove with its pipe disappearing into the gods and out of a distant window. The congregation were huddled around it like trappers from the Hudson's Bay Company. Thankfully the service was kept short, ending with the words "A Happy Christmas and many of them to you all!" from our Papas.

The twinkling lights from the kafeneon opposite, opened for the occasion, were invitation enough to the numbed flock and we all fell into its tiny but roasting interior. Petros and Maria buzzed about serving chipero and brandy and plates of hot chips, fried sausages and toasted bread. The children, who never seemed to tire, were lifted up to sit on the edge of the tables and were fussed over and talked to by everyone. Soon, with body and soul warmed, we got up to leave. Crossing the square in the cold, crisp night with the lights and happy hum of the kafeneon behind us, Vasilis said, contentedly, "Now this is what I call Christmas".

Winter... and Spring excursions

We saw the New Year in with Jo and Vasilis at a taverna in the nearby village of Dilofo. Eating out in Zagoria during the winter months is limited to the few isolated tavernas which remain permanently open. In Dilofo, a log fire greeted us in a small, square room; wood panelled walls, with knick-knacks haphazardly nailed on them, gave it the hint of an Alpine lodge. On a shelf, a rather sad and dusty stuffed fox, incongruously wearing a pair of horn-rimmed sunglasses, looked down on us. Two tables had been pushed together and laid out, and although the food, like the tavernas, was limited, it was superbly cooked on a grill laid across the glowing wood embers in the hearth. Soon wine flowed, the chipero bottle appeared and the landlord and his wife joined in. We all turned the meat, helped in the kitchen, poured more wine and played with the children. Songs were sung, sedately at first, then with more gusto and more out of tune as the evening wore on. Toasts to the year ahead were made at regular intervals and I felt certain that the fox, behind his dark glasses, was smirking at our antics.

By two in the morning the table was a shambles with the landlord nodding over his glass. The New Year was beginning to have a sinking feeling so we gathered ourselves together with coats, scarves, hats, children and toys, paid our bill with a generous tip and stepped out through the taverna door to meet it.

Heavy snow fell on New Year's Day. Huge, fluffy flakes – Christmas Card flakes – the type of snow I remember from being a small boy. Watching it from the window, and feeling about six years old, I was determined if enough fell to make myself a snowman. Then I thought, no, I'd make a snow-woman instead, and see Papa Kostas' reaction. By afternoon well over a foot had settled. Accompanied by strange looks from Effie I set to with a shovel and before long had built a life sized, truly voluptuous snow-woman. Towards evening, Papa Kostas and Elevtheria called round and there, in the courtyard, proudly stood my frozen Aphrodite. Kostas looked, fell back a pace, then going up to her reached out and fondly polished her shiny white boobs! "Kalos! Kaalloss!!" Very good! V-e-r-y good!! Elevtheria thought it a huge joke and the two of them, giggling conspiratorially, busily patted more snow onto her, turning her into a very obviously pregnant snow-woman!

They had called to ask us to go with them, for company, to light the three shrines that stand along the roadside going out of the village beyond the church. These little shrines are found all over Greece and are usually dedicated to some saint or another. Many are placed where a road accident occurred, put there by grieving relatives to mark the spot, or out of gratitude for a lucky escape. Often, on a dangerous corner, a cluster of shrines will be grouped together, far more effective as a warning than any road-sign. Wrapped up against the cold we trudged with them through the drifting snow, stars beginning to twinkle overhead as we reached the last shrine, Agios Yannis, half a mile away from the village. On our way home, coming round the final bend, we stopped with delight at the view of Koukuoli, nestling snugly against the dark hillside, lit by a scattering of random street lights sparkling frostily on rooftops thatched in white icing sugar.

Back in their warm kitchen, noses tingling, we were invited to share the ritual cutting of their New Year cake. Baked within it are five different items and whoever has the good fortune to find one in his slice will have the luck it represents for the rest of the year. A coin stands for wealth; a twig of Krania for strength; a vine leaf means a good grape harvest; a piece of straw, bread and food enough throughout the year; and lastly a ring for marriage. Effie and I drew blanks but Papa Kostas was extremely chuffed to get the vine leaf and on the strength of it topped up our glasses.

It continued to snow throughout the night and the car, by morning, was firmly trapped in our garden. It happened that our cigarette supply was running low so, armed with boots and walking sticks, muffled up with scarves and gloves, we set out to walk to Kipi, three miles through the forest. The first leg took us past the shrines, then left up a banking and onto the old trail that used to be the only link between the two villages. It was heavy going with the last night's snow fall but then, at the top of the climb, came our reward. As far as the eye could see, pine trees lay before us, encrusted with deep soft whiteness. Straining boughs laden with snow occasionally released their burden in a shower of white, windswept iridescence as a bird took flight at our approach. Below, in the valley beside the icy river lay Kipi, as silent and frozen as the landscape.

The path was not easy to follow and several times we wandered off course into a dead end of trees and bushes. Eventually we found our way to the top of the old steps that would take us down into the little gorge, Vikaki. Built over two hundred years ago and still in good preservation they zigzag steeply to the bottom where the river is crossed by a graceful stone bridge arching between cliffs of granite.

Kipi is a much larger village than Koukouli and is the administrative centre for our area, complete with police station and post office. As we approached, the threatening clouds broke open for a moment and the sun burst through. Kipi had taken on the air of a small ski resort. Yellow giant-tyred bulldozers were clearing the main road. Small boys were engaged in snowball fights, often throwing wide of the mark and hitting some unsuspecting adult, all evidence of the culprit vaporising behind a parked car. In the kafeneon, men were playing backgammon, and we were told that because of the snow and further forecasts of same, to help preserve stocks cigarettes were being rationed to two packs per person. Takis, a friend of four years standing, came in and we sat together warming ourselves round the stove. We had first met him on one of our original house hunting expeditions. A remarkably fit man in his late sixties who was, until recently, President of the Ioanninan Tennis Club and still plays tennis as often as he can. Takis was born in Egypt where about 250,000 Greeks had lived and worked for several generations. The Greek community got along very well with the British, who had held Egypt as a protectorate since 1914. However, when in 1956 all remaining British left the Canal zone under an agreement with Lieutenant Colonel Nasser (his title at the time), he promptly nationalised the Suez Canal and then slowly, by obstructive measures, eased the Greek population out of Egypt. A number of these Egyptian Greeks, whose families had originated from Zagoria, had inherited houses in Zagorian villages, and on their return to Greece, took them up again. All the Egyptian Greeks we have met here speak excellent English, very often French as well and are cultured, strongly motivated people with a wide range of interests.

Talking to Takis whiled away a good hour in the kafeneon and when we next looked out, snow was again falling heavily. We decided that we'd better get home pretty smartly, and rather than tackle the steps in blizzard conditions, set off along the main road. Although it had been cleared the snow had already settled an inch or more and the driving flakes stung our eyes. Squinting on our way, slithering in the slushy road, we arrived at the turn off where the track to Koukouli starts, and came upon Papa Kostas, Elevtheria and all the kids struggling to fit snow chains on the back wheels of their Lada. The Koukouli track had not been cleared and the tyre marks which Papa Kostas had made in the morning, taking the children to school, had already filled in. It was freezing cold and we didn't envy them the task, but there was little we could do to help and so, eventually, we left them to it. It took us nearly an hour to struggle home and our legs were aching from the effort of walking in deep, soft snow. Later we learned that it had taken Papa Kostas an hour and a half to get the car to the village. One thing was certain: there could be no question of going to school again whilst this weather lasted.

Some days later, with our car still garden-bound, we found we needed to stock up with basic vegetables, tinned foods and other supplies. The nearest shop to us was in Tsepelovo, ten miles away higher up the mountain. We were told that the bus from Ioannina stopped on the main road at the far end of Koukouli at four in the afternoon, calling at Tsepelovo and then going on to the next village where it turned around and set off back on the return journey. It would give us half an hour in Tsepelovo to do our shopping.

So, at ten past four we climbed aboard what, to our surprise, turned out to be a very smart, heated, luxury Mercedes bus, empty apart from two fellow passengers who got off at Kapesovo. To begin with the road was reasonably clear, but the higher we went the more it became covered with packed snow. The vast, sweeping windscreen wipers, acting like snowploughs, barely kept the screen clear. The driver seemed blissfully unconcerned with the conditions in which he was driving and spent most of his time shuffling through a stack of cassettes trying to find suitable music for the occasion. Gliding along we felt like two children allowed out alone for the first time. We sat up at the front with the driver and gazed in awe at the passing snow-clad scenery. It was dreamlike. We were floating in a giant glass bubble through a white wilderness. A large bird of prey wheeled effortlessly, eyeing our progress. A fox, desperate for food, peered at us over the top of a drift.

The bus stopped at the lower part of Tsepelovo and the driver said he would be back in half an hour, but would wait for us for a while if we weren't there absolutely on time. How effortless it was proving to be, bussing in Zagoria. So different from the agony of travelling on English buses, snarled up by bad weather with drivers and fellow passengers all out of temper. This was service, with a smile. Waving him off, we turned up the lane to the square.

The village shop-cum-taverna is run by Alex Gouris, a sprightly, elf-like man in his early sixties who has spent all his life in and around Tsepelovo and knows the mountains and old trails like the back of his hand. For years he guided all the walkers and climbers attracted to the area and some while ago, showing shrewdness and enterprise, he and his wife opened a small pension, successfully running it in what could well be described as organised slow motion. Although surprised to see us come stumbling into his shop on such a day, knocking the snow from our boots, he immediately had the whisky bottle and two glasses out on the counter. Alex speaks excellent English which he professes to have learned from listening to the B.B.C, and with his quick wit and wicked sense of humour it's always fun talking to him. He and I caught up on local news whilst Effie buzzed about getting together all the things we needed, piling them on the counter. Weighed and paid for, these purchases were stacked in her rucksack and Alex and I heaved it onto her back. I was given sole responsibility for a dozen eggs in a plastic bag, a division of labour to which I readily agreed.

Back in lower Tsepelovo, we were buying a newspaper for Papa Kostas from the kiosk, just as the bus came rolling round the corner, and we clambered once more into our private bubble. The return journey was made in gathering twilight and the street lights from distant villages sparkled in the frosty air like jewels on a cushion of blue-grey velvet.

We were having a late breakfast one morning, not long afterwards, when Papa Kostas, in cassock and stove pipe hat, suddenly burst into the kitchen. With his curling black hair and beard he appeared like a miniature Rasputin on the rampage! Swinging an incense burner and declaiming some religious incantation he dipped a sprig of oregano into a chased metal bowl which his eldest son, who accompanied him, was carrying, and proceeded to slosh us liberally over the head with Holy Water. When we and our breakfast were suitably soaked, he disappeared as suddenly as he'd arrived.

Wiping ourselves down after this whirlwind baptism, I said to Effie,

"What was that all about then?"

"I've no idea," she replied, picking bits of oregano out of her coffee. We couldn't find anything in our Greek diary to give us a clue so we ended up asking Kiki, who explained that it was the day of the Baptism of Christ and her father goes to everyone in the village and blesses them. I presume they had learned not to indulge in a late breakfast on January 5th. Shouts of protest from our neighbour, Vasilia, higher up the hill, told us that she too had been appropriately doused, and a cheerful Papas continued on his mission of drowning the rest of the village in the name of the Lord.

Vasilia is a dear old lady who spent many years with her husband living and working in Romania before coming back with him to Koukouli. Her house is a typical Zagorian mansion, square built, two stories high with windowless basements under the front elevation. Living alone since her husband's death she has allowed the house to fall into such a state of disrepair that it's become a race between her and it as to which will last the longest. An earthquake some years ago certainly didn't help and large cracks have appeared where the ceilings and walls should join. The upstairs rooms are no longer used and in winter, with their broken panes and missing windows, the stairwell resembles a de Havilland wind tunnel. A large, bare hallway with the pointing between the flagstones painted a bright gloss blue, has a long, hand-woven runner leading to the kitchen. Stooping under the low, wooden framed doorway you enter a room in which the poorest of Dickens' characters would have felt at home.

All along the right hand wall is a vast, open, arched,

inglenook fireplace, complete with spit mechanism and iron pot hooks. Inside to the left is the old, domed bread oven with its curved iron door. Looking up the chimney you see years of cobwebs which undulate and wave in the downdraught. One cracked and glazed broken window has an old stone sink sloping away for the water to drain out through an open hole beneath the window frame. A copper pipe with a brass tap poking out from the wall over the sink is the sole supply of water to the house. In winter, to prevent it freezing, Vasilia keeps it running day and night. Left of the sink, in the corner as you come in, there stands a wooden, Tardis like construction which, we discovered, houses her lavatory. There is no bathroom and she has no hot water.

Also leading off from the hallway is the front room where she lives and sleeps. Her Zagorian fireplace, with the mattresses either side taking up the entire run of the wall, has been blocked up, and a vintage wood-burner sits inconveniently in the middle of the room, positioned to catch your shins, its pipe wired to the ceiling running along and out through the chimney breast. There is a small tubular, formica topped table, covered with a cloth, on which sits a framed photograph of her and her husband; a big round alarm clock that ticks with resounding hollowness; and a black and white television with no horizontal hold. She lives alone in such conditions, battling with the cold in winter, water shortages in summer, arthritis and diabetes. All the village rally round to help her in whatever way they can, bringing in her wood, clearing snow, keeping her company. Maria, fulfilling her role as local medical officer, regularly checks her blood pressure. A doctor from Tsepelovo goes the rounds of the villages every other week, but Maria holds the fort meanwhile, and if he is needed in between times, she has the telephone to call him.

In the summer Vasilia enjoys the company of the shepherds' wives, all old friends, and she spends a good deal of time with Michalis and Fo-fo. We, for our part, get her bits of shopping whenever we go to Ioannina, and pay her a visit now and then particularly during winter which is a lonely time for her. Apart from general moans, the weather and her aches and pains, she's a cheery soul and often, seeing us in the garden from her window, shouts for us to go up and have coffee with her. In good weather she steps out every morning on a round of the villagers' homes, a familiar figure stumping along, bent over a stout stick, black cardigan drooping from one shoulder, left arm held firmly behind her back.

On one occasion, when she called to chat with us, we offered her a coffee and a small dish of nuts. I went back into the kitchen just for a moment and returned to discover an empty plate - the nuts had vanished.

"Well," I said to Effie when she'd gone. "She wolfed that lot pretty quickly!"

The next occasion she came, the same thing happened. On the third occasion I just caught sight of her, having put a handful into her mouth, tipping the remainder into her apron pocket!

"For later," she explained, sensing my eyes on her.

We're told she has money in the bank, it's just that she can't bear to part with any of it. And in her own way she's far from ungenerous, turning up with flowers cut from the garden, lettuces or tomatoes she has grown, and whenever we visit there's always a coffee and a piece of Turkish delight to be had.

One of the advantages, we had told ourselves, of moving to the mainland was that we would be in a much better position to travel and see so many interesting and historical places. Six months later, having worked continuously on the house, it dawned on us that apart from visiting the villages nearby we had, in fact, been nowhere and seen nothing. Consulting the map, we decided that Metsovo, a fully fledged township just beyond the eastern boundary of Zagoria, would be worth a visit.

The road to Metsovo climbs directly out of Ioannina on the eastern side of Lake Pamvotis and bends and turns its way up and over the southern reaches of the Mitsikeli range of mountains. Then it follows a winding ravine between Peristeri and the Pindos range. For nearly two hours the drive takes you through astounding scenery, but the road, though extremely well surfaced and maintained, is a gruelling and tortuous series of steep climbs and unfavourable cambers. Views abound on either side with gushing rivers, valleys and foothills clad in pine, pockets of cultivated plain and peaks of barren rock. Finally, climbing ever steeper, there is a momentary view of Metsovo, tumbling down a hillside.

It comes as a shock to see that almost all the roofs of the village are red tiled, not the stone of our western Zagorian villages, and the initial feeling is one of disappointment. The village itself is entered from the top, and the narrow high street with its wooden balconies and overhanging upper stories, stone walls and very Alpine character, descends steeply to the main cobbled plateia. From within the village the red roofs are out of view, and Metsovo undoubtedly has all the feel and charm of a hillside, mountain resort. In and around the village square are a series of old shuttered kiosks, of wooden construction, used as shops, kafeneons, a barber, and very simple restaurants. We parked Suzi under the comfortable shade of a lofty dark pine, close by.

On the way down we'd noticed an attractive looking hotel: all stone arches, wooden balustrading and shuttered windows, with the characteristic first floor overhang; so we walked back up to book a room before doing anything else. Inside was a handsome reception and lounge area, panelled in wood throughout, with a carved ceiling boasting vivid green and red cloth insets. The hanging lamps and wall brackets were intricately crafted in bronze and the wooden chairs and tables heavily worked and carved.

Metsovo is still very much the centre of the Vlachs, the once nomadic tribe of shepherds whose origins stem from Roman Legions based, during the Roman Empire, in what is now known as Romania. The people of Metsovo speak amongst themselves in an unwritten language akin to Romanian. Until the advent of the motor-car, the Vlachs, with their mule trains, virtually held a monopoly on transport within the Balkans and still are predominant in this trade, with lorries and trucks now as well as mules. Apart from shepherding they possessed many other skills, wood carving, weaving, tailoring, bootmaking and saddlery, all essential to nomadic sufficiency. They were expert blacksmiths and developed their talents into becoming excellent gold and silver smiths, renowned for their fine work to this day.

The flocks of sheep in Metsovo are small in comparison with the past, and the village has developed a more mixed economy, bolstered by tourism. A number of years ago, a ski-lift was installed providing simple skiing down gentle slopes, appealing very much to the novice. It is inexpensive and unflashy, catering for the unsophisticated amateur rather than high society showbiz skiers so well known from the glossy magazines of Northern Europe. Now that another piste, requiring greater skill, has been established, Metsovo is gaining in reputation as a worthwhile ski resort. This has brought visitors to the village and enables locals to display their weaving, jewellery, silverware and woodcrafts for sale, as well as their excellent cheeses and dairy produce. The villagers are proud of their heritage and skills, and many still go their daily round in traditional costume, which lends an authenticity and charm to the general scene.

The shops, we discovered, had lovely things for sale amongst the usual knick-knackery of tourism. There were beautifully designed hand-woven carpets, rugs and cushion covers in the deep and harmonious colours that natural dyes produce. Some shops professed to sell antique tapestries and rugs, but the stocks seemed so vast that I was not entirely convinced as to their actual antiquity. Certainly they looked old, but it's possible that having hung outside the shops for months on end in rain, dust and sunshine they had become prematurely antiqued. Nevertheless we did buy a loomed, light weight rug with a traditional motif in mulberry and bilberry on a black background - very moody. There were hordes of woodturned artefacts, bowls, spindles, balusters, but we stumbled across a workshop, tucked away in one of the back streets, that showed us what the true craftsman can do.

From outside it looked neglected, even tumbledown, with only a small sawdusty window in which a magnificently carved chest stood, dust strewn and seemingly forgotten. There was absolutely no other sign of what lay behind the closed wooden door. We let ourselves in to a small reception area with a counter barring the way. On it, two large ringbinders held coloured photographs of the work that the owner and his employees had produced. It was stunning. Carved throne-like chairs, chests, settles, tables, screens, lecterns, pulpits and a range of other ecclesiastical accessories. In the workshop behind, the men were deeply engrossed in carving an iconostasis ordered for a church in Athens. It was made up in sections and each craftsman was carving his with the aid of a finely detailed drawing. The entire piece would take over a year to complete, and they had a backlog of commissions that would keep them hard at work for three years or more.

Hungry by this time, we stopped at what turned out to be a 'slow food' kiosk in the square. Rotating on long spits over a charcoal grill was something quite unfamiliar to us and totally unrecognisable. However, we ordered two portions and sat down at a rickety table in front with our beers. Effie and I are not of the school that says 'I won't like it. I've never tried it.' When our order arrived, all of half an hour later, lukewarm and greasy in paper cones, we wished we had been! Although it smelled extremely appetising it was absolutely disgusting, utterly inedible and impossible to swallow. We chewed and we chewed, trying to make out to the stallholder that we thought it wonderful, whilst inwardly feeling sicker and sicker. A small plump dog with a knowing look plonked himself down beside us and stared expectantly up. Obviously foreign tourists were a dead ringer in this establishment and discreetly we palmed him the rest of our lunch, which he gobbled up enthusiastically.

Now that we had got rid of it we were intrigued to know what this extraordinary Greek delicacy consisted of, so we asked the chef. It is a dish called 'Kokoretsi' made out of offal: alternating pieces of liver, lights and lamb fat, threaded onto a skewer. Lambs intestines, which have been washed and turned inside out, are wound round and round to hold everything together and sprinkled with salt, pepper and oregano. The trick we were told, not that I could imagine any trick being required, was to allow this revolting mess to drain for two hours before spit roasting it. We went back to the hotel and lunched on plain salad and a plate of chips.

In the afternoon we found a small band had appeared in the square, and a circle of young teenagers in traditional costume were dancing to the local, Balkan-style music. The girls were attractively clad with the typical black embroidered aprons over long thick red skirts, and had their hair similarly tied up in scarves with coins sewn onto them. The boys wore short, full black pleated skirts and plain waistcoats over wide-sleeved blouses. All alike, they wore woolly white tights with tasselled gaiters below the knee and red, clog like shoes with black pom-poms on the toecaps. The Master of Ceremonies, a tall imposing figure of a man sporting a black handlebar moustache, wore the same outfit, with the addition of a wide tooled leather belt, a short flared cape slung over one shoulder and a jaunty black, pill-box hat. A beautifully curved sword in a chased silver scabbard swung nonchalantly from his belt against his left leg. With the aid of a swagger stick he oversaw the dancing and directed the band which consisted of a high pitched, shrieking clarinet, a drum and tambourine, an apparently untuned violin and a metal stringed bouzouki. The band stand was denoted by the semi circle of empty beer bottles at their feet.

Amongst the crowded spectators we noticed how

many of the older men with striking hawk-like faces and greying cavalier moustaches wore the pill-box hat, with a heavy cape or dark jacket slung across their shoulders. They all sat watching, leaning forward onto their glitsas. The dancing was delightful and all the various movements were followed and applauded with enthusiasm. We became aware that this must be some local celebration which, in all likelihood, would go on until the early hours of the following morning.

That evening, after dinner, we wandered down to have coffee in the square. The band had moved into a large hall close to where we had parked the car, and some merrymakers urged us to join the party. A drink was thrust into our hands and we stood to one side watching the locals cavort around the dance floor. The band was nearing its death throes. The music, indescribably bad, was suffering from a surfeit of beer. The immaculate Master of Ceremonies looked like a man who had taken on half the Turkish army single handed. His tights were muddy and wrinkled; the buckle on his ornate belt was halfway round his back and he kept tripping himself up on his sword; the pom-pom was missing from one of his shoes and his hat, now seriously misshapen, kept falling over his eyes. The swagger stick was being wielded in a dangerous fashion with onlookers ducking as he conducted his troops to the last.

Having visited Metsovo, we felt we should also go to Konitsa, just beyond the north western boundary of Zagoria. Konitsa is situated on the steep foothills of Mount Trapezitsa above the vast, flat plain created by the river Aoos at its confluence with the Voidhomatis, providing a wealth of fertile alluvial fields, laid out with irrigation channels, sluices and dykes. Lying close to the Albanian border, it was here in 1947-49 that the Greek Communist partisans tried, unsuccessfully, to capture Konitsa and establish it as the Communist capital on Greek soil. In the bitter fighting most of the original houses were destroyed, and we found that nearly all the buildings in Konitsa were of recent origin. The central square is right at the top of the village and to get there you must swing left and right for nearly a mile through blocks of modern apartments. Around the square there are a few older shops sprinkled between the newer buildings but basically Konitsa is a modern township with few architectural qualities. Below it, however, at the lower end of the Aoos Gorge, straddling the great river, is one of the largest single-arched bridges in the whole of Greece.

We had been advised to visit the Monastery of the Dormition of the Virgin belonging to a village with the unpronounceable name of Molyvdoskepasto which turned out, in fact, to be on the opposite side of the Aoos. This was confusing enough but, to make matters worse, maps of this area, so very close to the Albanian border, are kept deliberately vague for military reasons and ours was no exception. Correctly we took the road which runs from Konitsa back along the northern side of the Aoos. Climbing out of the valley, we descended once more to meet the river just before it flows into Albania. There is a rustic pontoon bridge here and a manned military post, neither of which detract from the very beautiful view. You look down into crystalline water flowing over flattened shelves of rock, through little ravines into wide open pools of pure turquoise with the leafy boughs of flowering ash dipping into them.

There was no doubt, according to the map, that to get to the monastery we should stay on our side of the bridge, taking the road to the right so, with the two gun-toting sentries eyeing us suspiciously, that's the way we went. Immediately round the corner, the road disintegrated into a rutted track. On and on we pressed through wooded rocky terrain, bumping and splashing through mud. Effie pointed out that there seemed to be a series of quaint little churches on rocky outcrops between the trees on the far side of the river, with strange horizontal windows. Perhaps they were shrines? Neither. They were pillboxes and if manned our progress was being followed by machine guns! A hamlet came into view which thankfully turned out to be Greek and a charming lady, hoeing her garden, explained that this was the end of the line. Despite the map we should have taken the road on the other side of bridge. We ran the gauntlet back past the 'quaint little churches' and a mile after crossing over the bridge, found the monastery.

Virtually moated by a bend in the river, it is set in a high walled enclosure amongst the trees. The church itself is thought, by the design of the apse, the tall octagonal dome and transverse barrel roof over the nave, to date from the 13th Century, but the site has been of religious significance since the 7th Century. It is an enchanting building with walls a random mixture of stone and old brick giving them a warmth of colour against the various rooflines of dark grey stone. The octagonal dome, nearly the height of the building again, is capped with a round, conical stone roof. To the left, round two sides of a flagged courtyard, are the dormitories built over arched storehouses, the upper verandah railings covered with a wonderfully prolific and fragrant wisteria. The stones are whitewashed, the little cells spotless and there is, overall, a feeling of peace and sanctity.

A tall Papas materialised from around a building and glided towards us. Appreciating we were English, he led us into the church, gently pointing out all its features, telling us of the history and holiness of all the various artefacts. The door was made from two huge chunks of dark oak, each divided into three panels and finely carved with griffin and saintly figures. Inside was damp and musty and sadly many of the wall paintings were damaged.

Coming out into the sun again, we were led into a stone roofed portico where booklets, pamphlets and postcards were neatly displayed, together with reproductions of the icons. Naturally everything was in Greek, some tracts even in ancient Greek, but we bought anyway as a way of repaying our courteous guide. One postcard we didn't buy showed the double electrified fence, not a hundred yards away, marking the boundary between Albania and Greece, which struck an ugly and discordant note in a place of such peace.

Coming home by a different route, along the spine of a ridge separating two plateaux, we stopped to watch three pairs of Golden Eagles majestically soaring, from one side to the other, playing the thermals. By nature of the land we were almost on a level and could watch them closely without binoculars - a rare and wonderful experience.

Easter – Rebuilding begins

Evidence of Easter approaching was best observed at Papa Kostas' house. A fine spring afternoon and the whole family were busily and noisily engaged in redecorating. The kitchen, normally the centre of their day-to-day activities, was stripped and the old wood-burning stove already repainted in fireproof silver. Kiki was washing and cleaning all the pictures and ornaments, the curtains were blowing on the line and Papa Kostas had just finished painting the ceiling. On entering this scene of activity I was greeted with unusual warmth and instantly sensed that I, too, was destined to become involved.

"Ah! Just the man!" exclaimed Papa Kostas, pouring me a glass of his now drinkable though heady wine.

"I've bought a new cooker extractor but I need some help. The problem, you see," he continued, "is that the old one is too low down and really I want the new one to be higher up. But it'd mean we'd have to cut and modify the cupboards above wouldn't we?"

I agreed that we would and so, whilst Papa Kostas got on with painting the kitchen walls, I modified the cupboards.

Hours later, after endless trips up and down the lane to my workshop for one tool or another, I had them finished. By this time the rest of the family had gone to bed.

"All we need now is a few tiles to finish it off," Kostas said enthusiastically, and with a torch we delved into one of his outhouses. Having shifted most of its contents we found a small stack of the original tiles in a dusty corner. Back home I went, for the tile cutter and some glue, and it wasn't until one o'clock in the morning we finally stood back to admire our efforts.

"I've another little job," he said, just as I was leaving, "but I'll tell you about that tomorrow. Goodnight, and thanks!"

Next day - bedlam reigned. All interior doors were out in the courtyard being blow-torched of their old paint. Kristo, the eldest son, was painting shutters; Elevtheria was reorganising the bathroom; their paint spattered dog had retired to a safe place; and Papa Kostas had started on the main bedroom upstairs. The television was sitting on top of a chest of drawers and with a sweeping arm movement he said, "The idea is to move this chest out onto the landing and make floor-to-ceiling shelves for our books. I'd like to make a big shelf for the television with cupboards underneath. What d'you think?"

Foolishly I said I thought it was a very good idea.

"What wood d'you suppose I'll need and do you think your friend Apostolis could cut it for me?"

For the next half hour we measured and discussed Papa Kostas' timber requirements.

"Right. I'll get all that in Ioannina tomorrow and then we can get cracking!"

By lunchtime next day the timber was leaning against the outhouse.

"Well?" said Papa Kostas, seeing me inspecting the wood. "When do we start?"

We started then and there. I went back to my

workshop and brought down all the tools I thought would be needed and, with loud Zagorian music playing on the local radio station, we set to and built the shelves that afternoon. I prefer to use screws and take my time over such a project. Papa Kostas prefers to use an assortment of rusty nails and time, for him, is at a premium. I lent him a tin of woodstain I happened to have in stock and later, when I saw the final result with splatters from the brush on his freshly painted walls, I came to realise that detailed work was not for him. This man was strictly a builder - tons of sand, bags of cement and a pile of stones were more his style.

Through Holy Week Papa Kostas, wearing his ecclesiastical hat, works like a Trojan. Every day he gives a two and a half hour service either in Koukouli or Kapesovo and on the more important occasions in both. The service on Good Friday, in the evening, is one of the most picturesque and well attended. The church in Koukouli is packed, our numbers bolstered by the temporary return of the summer people who come to celebrate Easter in their village. The church is fully lit, the chandeliers glow and glitter, the large brass candelabra are ablaze and everyone carries a lit candle throughout the service. Even the smallest toddler has one and some of the older women in black have fistfuls of them. In the centre of the nave stands an intricately carved, wooden pergola densely decked with flowers, containing an icon of Christ, representing the bier with the body of Christ upon it. Dirges are sung continuously, led by Papa Kostas. Standing in the aisles, in the nave, on the steps, everyone sings without the accompaniment of any musical instrument, following from small books.

After two hours of ceaseless singing, the bier is

lifted from its table and carried out on the shoulders of four men through the main door, preceded by Papa Kostas and two men carrying ornate lanterns on long poles, a third man carrying aloft a bejewelled, silver cross. The congregation follow with all their candles into the night and the procession solemnly walks around the village singing dirges all the way. Stopping at the most Eastern, Northern and Western points of the village, where blessings are delivered, we all troop behind with our glittering candles which I am convinced must be specially made for the occasion by an offshoot company of The Dry Cleaners' Federation of Greece. Hot wax drips everywhere - onto the backs of people in front, onto your shoes, onto your own back from someone behind!

Finally, arriving once more at the church, the Papas leads his flock to the South facing door which is closed. The bier is held up at head height and the Papas knocks three times on the door demanding it be opened. Twice from inside the reply is a refusal, but on the third request the door is flung open and the Papas, followed by everyone else, passes under the bier to re-enter the church. With the opening of the door it is understood that Christ has been accepted into heaven and will rise again. The joyousness of the final singing once everyone has re-gathered is felt with tremendous force, and the Papas' final blessing, deeply moving.

On Easter Saturday, the service is held from ten o'clock through to midnight, and on the stroke of midnight the church bells are frantically rung to herald the risen Christ. "Kristos Anesti" Christ is risen, and "Alithos Anesti" He is truly risen, can be heard on all sides whilst in joyous mood everybody returns to their homes to sit en famille, and break their Lenten fasting with a bowl of the special Easter soup which they have prepared in readiness. We had seen Elevtheria's pot of boiling offal being scooped free of thick grey scum only two days before, the first stage of the soupmaking process, and politely declined their insistent invitations to join them.

Preparations for Easter, which is by far the most important celebration in the Greek calendar, had been going on for weeks in every household, particularly for the Easter Sunday luncheon, eaten after yet another two hour church service. Special bread and Easter biscuits had been baked, thousands of eggs boiled and dyed and the lamb or kid prepared for spit roasting. Sunday dawned a gloriously sunny day and behind his house, in a meadow bursting with spring flowers, Papa Kostas had set up his stall. An electric cable looped out of the kitchen window and across the outhouse roof down to a lashed up motor on a ramshackle spit that falteringly rotated, bearing the trussed and larded carcass of a goat, complete with head. Nearby a bonfire of logs blazed and from this spadefuls of glowing embers were transferred to the spit keeping the cooking heat constantly at the right pitch. He and Elevtheria had made an early start since the goat would take a good six hours to cook thoroughly.

Now with the service over, and in casual wear, Kostas was busy basting the goat and replenishing the bonfire. Meanwhile, children and friends brought out other food, chairs, tables and large carafes of wine. Two of the boys lay in the grass playing chess, occasionally breaking off to give each other a noisy pummelling. The radio was playing folk music and by eleven the dancing and drinking had begun. It was a wonderful setting for a party, and we sat under a blossoming quince tree taking it all in: the dancing, the children, the grown-ups' preoccupation with the spit, and the family dog sitting bolt upright watching it revolve with an expectant concentration. The view across the wooded hillside down to the Gorge gave this idyllic setting a fantastic backdrop and we wouldn't have been surprised to turn round and find pagan Pan sitting under a tree, playing his pipes in the shade, as happily a part of the scene as we were.

Greek hospitality is renowned and we had been invited to several Easter Day celebrations, starting with Papa Kostas, and it was clear that a certain amount of self control was going to have to be brought to bear if we were to remain in any way sober. Kostas and the family urged us to stay on until the goat was cooked well enough for us to have a slice. But we simply couldn't - we knew the little creature too well! From a small kid, born just before Christmas, we'd watched him being bottle fed by Elevtheria in their kitchen. He'd nibbled our finger ends, butted the cat, sat on our laps to be petted and performed playful leaps to escape the children. Only two weeks before, getting into our garden over the wall at the back, he'd managed to jump onto the roof of the house. From the workshop I'd heard frantic bleatings in two tones; the deep throated mother from street level at the front of the house, and the kid from the apex of the roof two stories up, teetering on the edge. Papa Kostas' family's Easter Lunch!!!

"Effie! Efffieee!! Quick! HELP!!"

Unknown to me she'd decided to trade some English curled parsley for some fresh spring onions and was away across the village out of earshot. I dashed out of the workshop and pounded round the garden to get to the back of the house in time to lure him off the roof. Fortunately I succeeded and returned the little blighter to his mother. There was really no way now that I could eat him!

We moved on, but passing a household further down the street the owner, whom we had not yet met, insisted that we join him and his family for a drink. We stayed an hour or more then, on our way again, spotted the tell-tale smoke from a courtyard ahead. Desperate not to get involved in yet another unsolicited offer of hospitality, we surreptitiously took a detour up a side street and by using such tactics managed to stay more or less upright through the day.

Our final visit was to Petros and Maria, calculated to be the last on our schedule since from there it was simply a matter of falling over the wall to be home. Their two teenagers, back from university, and a clutch of relatives had set up the spit inside an open fronted outhouse in the courtyard. A long, makeshift table had been cobbled together from planks of wood and an old door, all disguised by a cheerful checked tablecloth. To keep hunger at bay until the main meal was ready, the table had been laid with bread, salads, Easter biscuits and a huge bowl of hardboiled eggs, dyed red. These eggs are a traditional part of Greek Easter and are used in much the same way as we play with conkers. One person grips an egg in their fist, pointed end up, while another gives it a smart tap with his egg. Whoever's egg cracks is the loser, the winner going on to challenge other comers. The cracked eggs are peeled and eaten, and before long everybody ends up with red fingers and a glut of peeled eggs, but it's a nice piece of nonsense to while away the time.

By mid-afternoon, when we arrived, they had finished their main meal and were settling down to coffees and brandy. We happily accepted a strong, black Greek coffee and our refusal of brandy was courteously ignored. Full of food from other visits and wishing for no more, diplomatically it was impossible to refuse Maria's homemade 'karidopita', small sticky cakes swimming in honey and encrusted with crushed walnuts. By five o'clock when we finally staggered home, not a sound could be heard in Koukouli. The village had eaten and drunk itself to sleep.

Easter over, life settled back into its normal, quiet routine. Most of the internal work on our house was completed and, with the fine spring weather, our thoughts began to turn to the garden. The stone wall just down our lane had collapsed during the winter and would have to be rebuilt, and others around the garden were seriously in need of repair from years of neglect. This was a priority since one of our biggest problems was keeping out the village sheep and goats. They had habitually taken a short cut over a low part of the wall, reducing it gradually to a heap of rubble, and cropped their way to another gaping hole at the back of the garden. On top of this, the front of the house was open to the lane since Mitsos had knocked down our original gate to make way for his bobcat. Trying to chase the sheep out was an exhausting circular marathon of frustration.

The need to close ourselves in became more urgent when, arriving home from town one day, we found all our potted plants around the verandah and down the steps severely pruned and a trail of thousands of visiting cards left behind. I have watched these creatures for hours and am totally convinced that the only colour they see is green. They zap from one green spot to another, their beady eyes scanning the next assault while strimming the first. In addition to the sheep, because we were without a gateway, we often found people wandering, reasonably enough, up the lane and into our garden without realising that it wasn't a continuation of the lane.

I discussed the building of a Zagorian lychgate with Papa Kostas. I was going to have a go at repairing the walls myself but thought a roofed lychgate was a little over-ambitious for a beginner. Since we had drawn up plans with Eleni for the conversion of the other house into a four-bedroomed, country hotel, we realised that any gateway must be made wide enough for Mitsos to drive his bobcat through when work on it began. So first I had to go and measure the machine and then, with Kostas, we planned the width and depth of the supporting walls and worked out what materials would be required. Although he couldn't start for the next two months he suggested we might just as well get everything we needed now. Prices, he said, would only go up if we left it until later.

Everything has to be brought to the village from Ioannina, and transport is by far the most expensive item. Two tons of sand are a third of the cost of its delivery and he was all for using the lorry and its driver to the best advantage. He would arrange for him to drive up with sand and ten bags of cement which would be dumped in the open area in front of the church. Then he would send him to pick up four tons of stones from the quarry several miles away and have them brought back to Koukouli. His logic was admirable. Whilst you have the lorry in Koukouli use it on local runs for other materials. When our house was being built by remote control from Corfu, all we had wanted was to see it finished and habitable, and we had not really been in a position to consider such details. But now we were living here we were becoming more street wise and beginning to see that considerable savings could be made.

Several days later the lorry arrived; sand, cement and stones were delivered, the driver paid, and we set to work in Suzi to haul it all up, load by load, to the house. It was ant work and at first the piles and heaps in front of the church looked formidable. But there's something very satisfying about watching the original piles dwindle, while the new ones gradually grow larger until you seem in the end to have more than you started with.

After that I began work on the wall down the lane. A quiet lane normally, but once the locals spotted me heaving stones about, it became busy with people and advice. Advice that I happily attended to since they had been building stone walls for generations. Dry stone walling is a skill that takes years to master, so I opted to bind the stones with cement, which I grouted out deeply when semi-dry. With this method the new part of the wall would more or less blend in with the old. It was slow, cumbersome work but after a week the street wall was back up, sanctioned by my most frequent visitors, Petros and Papa Kostas.

A little further up the lane, just outside where our new gate would be, was another landslide. This was a double skin wall, infilled with rubble and small stones and it occurred to us that it could be made into a flower bed rather than just solid wall. So the top part was left open, filled instead with good earth, and planted with bulbs, clumps of alpine primroses and creeping thyme from the wild. The street had become less busy after my first efforts and I was left in relative peace to get on with the job. Another week gone, and I was faced with the daunting task of tackling the long, forty yards or more of wall that stretched and weaved its way in front of our two houses. Nearly all this had to be built up another three feet to be effective and the end part, to the corner, entirely rebuilt from scratch as this was where the 'green-eyed' sheep had been zooming in for their fast food.

The previous two walls had been set into banking but this one was above ground, free standing and two feet thick. After my first day I looked at the result of my efforts and then way down to my ultimate destination. An aerial shot of The Great Wall of China sprang to mind - it was going to take a lifetime to get to the other end! Then the weather took a dive. No sooner would I get a dollop of cement mixed and ready to use than it would rain. These hold ups were unbearable and the wall seemed to be getting visibly longer by the day instead of shorter. Eventually in desperation I got our massive, bright blue, garden brolly, stuck it into the earth and worked under that, moving it along as I progressed.

Grouting was a boring job and gave me grouter's wrist which was very painful, but it had to be done before the cement set. Stuck under my parasol one wet evening, I was very pleased to hear Papa Kostas' familiar whistle as he approached up the lane. Passing the kitchen he called to Effie for two chiperos and joined me. He was fed up with not being able to get on with his jobs for the rain, and had come to see what I was up to. We stood together, blue-faced under the brolly, sipping our chiperos, haphazardly pecking away at the grouting, having a good healthy moan about the weather. It could have been any normal evening in a garden in England.

After a month I was just over two thirds of the way along and nearly up to the mulberry tree. By now it was early June and hot, and I was grateful for the shade. The next part would be even harder to do because this was where I was going to have to completely rebuild the wall. Petros and Maria, like their sheep, had got used to taking a short cut through here to the upper regions of the village, in addition to which they delivered our post over the wall. We felt it would be un-neighbourly to block it off altogether, so we put in a small gate made from an old wooden door with hammerhead nails, which we'd found kicking about in the garden amongst the nettles.

In this corner Mitsos had previously dug out a septic tank with his bobcat and had left a terrific mess. We filled and levelled the area, reclaiming piles of stone in the process. By now we reckoned we'd shifted several tons of stone by hand and at one time had borrowed a wheelbarrow, thinking it would help. But Greek wheelbarrows seem to be hewn from a solid lump of steel, weigh a ton when empty and are designed for short people with even shorter legs. We simply couldn't handle the thing, so we scoured Ioannina for a lightweight model and, Sod's law being what it is, eventually found one long after we'd finished all our stone humping. It was strong, super-light, had a wheel bar for tipping - the Greek ones don't, so you have to tip them sideways at a swinging trot - and just happened to be painted in exactly the same blue as our windows. A colour co-ordinated, streamlined wheelbarrow which Papa Kostas scornfully refers to as my 'Volvo Turbo', but is forever sending his sons to the house to beg the use of it.

With the stones we had unearthed, I built a wall around the bole of the mulberry tree, creating a flower bed, and shallow steps up to 'Petros' Gate'. I had a notion now about this corner. A small, hillocky, English lawn would not look out of place and it would make a change from endless flagstones. So we raked, de-stoned, raked again and sifted some beautiful fine soil on top of our lawn site. We watered and fed it and let it settle for the night.

Next day I was carefully casting grass seed when I caught sight of Petros' baseball cap over the top of the gate.

"What's that?" he asked.

"Grass seed," I replied.

"What for?"

"To make a lawn."

"What for?"

"To look at."

"But what for?"

This conversation was becoming repetitive and I could see a total lack of understanding beginning to develop. To have grass and no sheep was completely incomprehensible to Petros, and he nodded his head and the peak of his hat in despair. Staring solemnly at my would-be lawn, and then up at the sky, he made some comment about the weather and disappeared from view.

The seed cast, more fine earth sifted, carefully pressed down and watered, I sat on the steps and was able already to envisage a swath of 'Old England'. Being a person who likes immediate results, first thing in the morning I was out to inspect the lawn. To my disappointment not much had happened overnight, but I suddenly noticed a tiny movement, then... hundreds of them! A column of ants was busy carting away individual grass seeds. I couldn't believe it! At the rate they were going my little bit of Old England would be completely transplanted a foot underground in next to no time. Something had to be done - but what? I watched the ants with certain admiration for their dogged industry, but that wouldn't save my lawn. What if I put a handful of seed outside their nest, would that distract them? I poured a cupful around the nesthole and by next morning it was obvious their foreman had worked out some basic logistics, and decided it was better for his troops to move the pile nearby first and get back to the lawn later. I had to feed the ants for several weeks, hoping that Petros would not discover me in this new act of lunacy, until brave new shoots started to show through, but at least the ants 'Kept off the Grass'.

After church one Sunday, Papa Kostas turned up at the house with an array of hammers and stone cutting chisels. Selecting a few stones from our pile, he hunkered down like a garden gnome and chinked away at them for the rest of the day. This was the slow part of our gate construction, facing enough stones on two sides to give a good, straight edge. Each stone was examined, turned and hefted before the hammer struck. It was fascinating to watch him, and the concentration he put into the task gave it an almost ritualistic quality. When he was satisfied he had enough prepared, the actual building started. Together we marked out the base lines with string and spirit levels, cement was mixed, and the two walls began to grow.

Each evening, after Kostas left, we grouted out the stones so that these walls would match the others, and a week later our gateway stood resplendent. To recreate a Zagorian lychgate roof, Kostas built up two platforms of stone on the gate ends of the walls to carry four heavy beams across the span. Then the roof trusses were cut and nailed into position and flat planks hammered into place across them. To make the beams look older, we burned them with a blow torch, roughened them up with a wire brush and stained them. The finishing touch was the stone slates which we stripped off the roof of the old house. The completed gateway looked magnificent and Papa Kostas was as pleased as we were with the work.

The next part of the operation was mine, to make two doors in the style of old ones we had seen. They were each going to be one metre twenty five wide and two metres tall, so needed to be fairly substantial. I consulted Apostolis who came up with some excellent Swedish pine that normally would be cut and used as floorboards, but to be strong enough the gates needed planks twice the thickness of standard boarding, so these would be ideal. However, it meant that the setting of one of their machines would have to be altered and Apostolis volunteered to cut them for me on a Sunday when the factory was closed.

As Suzi struggled up the mountain with this load of timber I seriously began to wonder whether the finished doors might prove too heavy, so when I had sawn all the planks to length, I weighed one on the bathroom scales. Multiplying that by the number of planks per door I discovered that each one was going to weigh over 100lbs, without all the cross-ties, spars and well over forty bolts! The hinges I had already bought were not going to be up to the job.

The backstreets of Ioannina are full of small, family-run industries where they are willing to make up practically anything on a one-off basis. I found myself a metal workshop and told the man there about my problem. Nodding to himself he delved into the back of a long shelf of odds and ends and produced samples of hinges for me to choose from. He forged me six massively strong ones within the day and I came home praising Ioannina to the skies.

"I bet you'd be hard pushed to get that done in England nowadays" was becoming a common refrain.

The wooden gateposts were up, hefty chunks well bolted into the stone. I assembled the doors just inside the courtyard because it would be impossible for me with Effie to carry them any distance. Then, heaving them into position with chocks and props to stop them falling over, we fixed the hinges, first one door then the other. The worst moment came when we removed all the supports... to find, with a huge sigh of relief, that they swung open perfectly, and the hinges held.

Michalis and Fo-fo had recently replaced their rotten, worm infested front doors, and offered them to us as a means of getting rid of them. We jumped at the chance. Not for the doors themselves, they had to be hacked up and burned, but for all the old metal fittings, particularly the great black lock with its key nearly a foot long. Our new gates now proudly carry all these old fitments and closing them at night with the huge heavy key making a loud 'CLONK!' has a finality and sense of security that a Yale lock will never possess.

With the gate, and the walls almost finished, we had considerably reduced the goat and sheep activity in the garden. The hens had long given up. With wings going like windmills they had, several times, crash landed from the top of the wall and then found there was no way back. The cockerel, a typical macho type, had been more cautious but finally he got his comeuppance. Seeing one of his brides vanish squawking over the edge, he lifted his head and let out with a series of strident crows, as much as to say, "YOU STUPID SILLY BITCH!"

At this height of arrogance he completely lost balance, fell off the wall, and forgetting to flap his wings landed with an undignified thud. Slightly dazed and ruffled, he quickly regained his composure and standing on one leg glared at me. I opened the gate and with his head held high he led his clucking harem off the premises, never to return.

We still had the hole in the garden wall behind the house and all my attempts to barricade it with old doors and bits of wood had proved ineffectual with our 'green-eyed' friends. We had the plans submitted to build a proper workshop and storeroom there for when we had the hotel, but with the sheep constantly breaking and entering I couldn't see why we shouldn't build up the back wall onto the lane now, and finish the rest later on. Papa Kostas was beginning to find my Sheep Persecution Complex funny, partly I suspect because it was our garden they were invading not his, and partly because of my concern for our mystical lawn. His attitude changed dramatically however when I had to rush into their kitchen one day to warn him that "several goats, I think they're yours, are grazing in your allotments!"

Never have I seen a man move so fast. His coffee cup landed on the kitchen table, spinning, and in one sublime gymnastic movement he was on his feet and out of the door. With legs pounding like pistons he tore off down the lane, over rocks and piles of sand to the allotment where three goats, eyeing his arrival, were unhurriedly finishing their salad. On entering the allotment Papa Kostas, by force of habit, made a serious tactical error. He closed the gate behind him. Leaping into the arena he cursed and shouted, waved his arms and lobbed stones at the goats to drive them out. But to where? The gate was shut. Realising his error, he calmed down, opened the gate and gently shooed them out and the goats, neatly filching a few more lettuce leaves on the way, gave him a look of complete contempt.

When next I talked to him about building up the back wall, ready for the storerooms, he was very sympathetic. A changed man.

"Must keep the animals out of the garden - do enormous damage. A complete nuisance, you can't grow a thing!"

His actual urgency on the matter also surprised me because, by afternoon, he had organised three Albanians, who were living rough in the village, to help him with the labouring.

Since the fall of Hoxha and the Communist regime in Albania, we have been witness to much of what has been happening between Albania and Greece. That part of Albania which borders Greece, running west to the Adriatic coast was, originally, a part of Epirus and the people are still considered to be Epirotes. Their first language is Greek and they adhere to the Greek Orthodox Church, but since 1913 they have been geographically and politically Albanian. Greece offered visas and permits for Albanians to live and work in Greece, but these cost money and depended on the applicant's suitability. The majority of Albanians were without money and unable to prove their suitability, so many started to trudge on foot over the mountains and enter the country illegally in an endeavour to find a better life for themselves.

They came wearing the only clothes they possessed, often unshod, carrying their meagre belongings in a pillowcase slung over their shoulders. Those who were skilled in the art of stonemasonry and were Greek speaking Epirotes tended to stay in the villages, living rough, repairing and restoring buildings, labouring, turning their hands to anything that paid them. They stayed and worked, albeit illegally, for the summer and trekked back to their families in winter with their hard-gotten Greek drachmas. Others would press on, heading for the cities, hoping to submerge themselves in anonymity there, seeking bright lights and a better life.

Papa Kostas had negotiated the conditions of employment. Each would be paid 2,000 drachmas a day and be given two meals, for which he would work ten hours. Kostas and Elevtheria would feed and pay them and charge us accordingly when the work was done. The actual terms struck us as positively mediaeval. It was sheer exploitation. But we had to tell ourselves that given their situation it was in fact benefitting them; that we were living in a foreign environment where we were not in a position to dictate policy. Better to do what we could by providing them with coffees and cans of beer and throw in sandwiches and whatever else we could, as a bonus.

Progress on the wall was good but on the third day it poured with rain. Papa Kostas took the opportunity to go to Ioannina but the three ragged, sad-looking Albanians dutifully turned up for work. Since we had no idea what arrangements Kostas had made with them, whether he had told them to work or not, we didn't like to interfere. Through the early part of the morning the rain slackened off, then poured, eased, and poured again. Our three doggedly worked on, sheltering in the old house whenever the rain became torrential, but by eleven o'clock their predicament had become intolerable. They were getting soaked to the bone and had no change of clothes and no means of drying the ones they had on, so I went out and told them to stop working and I would pay them for a full day just the same. To my amazement they shook their heads and elected to continue. Back indoors, Effie asked me how I had got on.

"But WHY? It's madness for them to go on working in this!"

After a long, glum silence, she suddenly cried, "I've got it! If they don't work they don't get any food. Go and tell them to stop working NOW, and I'll get then a hot meal."

She cobbled together vast platefuls of mashed potatoes, bacon, sausages and fried eggs, which were eaten in the basement of the old house in total silence. Not a scrap was left. I paid them, gave them fruit, a loaf of bread and tins of sardines for afterwards, and they finally left.

The following day, cloudless, sunny and dry, produced Papa Kostas and the Albanians looking much more cheerful. They worked on and by six o'clock our wall was up and finished. We brought out chipero and beers to celebrate this moment of achievement.

At last a garden free of sheep and goats. Or, so we thought. Sitting outside reading a letter one morning, I thought I could hear a funny, familiar, munching noise and there, on top of the wall stood a goat, reaching up and hacking away with razor teeth at our only vine! I lobbed a stone at him and he ran away bleating.

Later in the day, Petros came round to ask me to jig out a piece of wood for him. Watching me in my workshop he suddenly said, "Did you throw a stone at one of my goats this morning?"

I had to admit that I did. "But it was only a small one."

"If you throw a stone at my goats another time," he said, "make sure it's a big bastard so they know who's in charge!"

With that he picked up a block of wood off the floor about the size of a house brick.

"THIS sort of size," he went on enthusiastically. "They don't understand pebbles!"

To give the vine a chance I made a low wooden fence along the top of the wall, just enough to prevent the goats from climbing up. The spars have a slightly Turkish shape to them, and stained grey, it actually enhances the wall. We think we've got it cracked at last because we've been free of 'green-eyes' for some time, but I still get a nervous twitch of apprehension whenever I hear their bells tinkling close by.

Walking the Vikos Gorge

Corfu boasts a magnificent 18-hole golf course with probably the finest greens in Europe and it is, as one golfing correspondent put it, 'Europe's Best Kept Secret'. To me, walking in the company of friends on a carpet of lush green, leisurely bashing a ball into a distant hole on a virtually deserted links, is perfect relaxation. But to Effie it is a totally bewildering activity. No more bewildering, however, than I find her love of setting out with her friend Ann for a long day hike to a destination that is served perfectly adequately by a bus! Every Thursday, when we lived on Corfu, I took myself off to the Golf Club whilst those two disappeared on some marathon trek.

In winter they would walk the coastline, cutting inland and back again to windswept coves. Out of season the beach tavernas and bars were closed, the pedalos, speedboats and tripper caiques all put to bed to await another season of fun and noise. But in summer the tourists drove them off the coastal paths and, like a couple of migrating birds, they wandered instead deeper inland among the hills and villages that tourism, so far, had passed by.

Ann and her husband had arrived on Corfu in their boat 'Explorer' thirty years ago. They loved the island so much that they decided to stay and bought a small cottage up in the hills overlooking the sea. Ann is a leading botanist, an authority on the countless wild flowers of the Mediterranean and has made sporadic trips to various parts of Greece, and its many islands. But her confessed first love is for the mountains and hills of Zagoria.

Whilst we were still on Corfu, Effie spotted an advertisement in a magazine for a small English travel company who had started to organise walking holidays in Zagoria. Hot foot she took this up to show Ann and having sent off for their brochure, the pair of them spent hours sifting through the jungle of incomprehensible information unique to travel brochures and railway timetables alike, and discovered that they could join the group at their starting point in Monodendri. They booked up and in due course, like a couple of excited schoolgirls, with packed rucksacks drove to the mainland in Ann's car. This was the first of many such expeditions which have taken them through some of the most beautiful, wild and often awe inspiring territory in Europe. And in retrospect, it was a brilliant exercise in research and development since Effie met and made contact with people who, after we came to live here, proved good friends and were of invaluable help.

On their first morning, waking at the crack of dawn to organise themselves and get togged up, they set off with their guide, Kostas Vasileiou, to descend into the Vikos Gorge. It was raining, the mist swirling round rocky pinnacles as they followed a steep and ragged goat path into the depths of the ravine. The trees dripped and grasses were bowed over with heavy droplets. Spiders' webs hung white and waterlogged by the wayside. It was absolutely still, and the single cry of a bird echoed alarmingly from the rock faces. At the bottom, after an hour's descent, Kostas called a brief halt in the dried out, stony riverbed, thick with willow.

As they walked further and further down the Gorge, the rain eased off. The mists lifted and patches of blue sky appeared, high up between the walls of the canyon where flurries of chough swirled and chattered. Out of the riverbed they climbed through airy woodlands of aspen and poplar, trunks soaring and thin in an attempt to grow towards the light. Then they came to a flat land, way above the river bed which was wider now with monolithic boulders holding deep still pools of trapped, black water. Much larger trees grew here - thick trunks blackened with moss, growing in tortuous shapes. Dead branches hung at grotesque angles dangling lichen like rotting flesh; vast rocks covered in ferns, fungus and moss reared up between the trees but no light got through and nothing could be seen beyond. It had a grim and fairy-tale atmosphere and it was here they saw their first spotted salamander, a weird and primeval lizard-like creature, as black and shiny as wet liquorice with startling bright-yellow dashes of colour.

Down they went under a great shelf of overhanging rock festooned with thick ivy, its age old stems protruding like swollen veins on arthritic hands. Bramble tendrils tugged at them as they pressed on, climbing quite steeply to a sudden grassy sward in the open, a pincushion of turf atop a rocky prominence with unsurpassable views up and down the Gorge. The sun had broken through, birds had begun to sing, insects hummed, and they halted for a while to sit, take a drink, absorb the scenery and the atmosphere of such a secret and lonely location.

Back on the trail they scrambled across miles of steep scree, descending to kinder terrain as the Gorge widened out. Now they could see both sides, with towering configurations of stone forms like a set from some fabulous mythological opera, and looking up to the cliff tops etched against the sky at neckbreaking height, they appreciated the enormity of the chasm in which they stood dwarfed and insignificant.

Stopping for lunch in a conveniently boulder strewn field hemmed in with trees, they delayed long enough to realise that the mists were returning, driving back up the Gorge towards them, so they shouldered their backpacks and set off once more. Slowly, as the valley opened, the cliffs on the left became more tame, and those on the right more massive and awesome. They were approaching the more northerly facing Towers of Papingo. The river was still dried out but bordered by plane trees and eventually they ended up leaving the trail, which led to the village of Vikos, and carried on walking down the riverbed. There is an astonishing sight, just below the start of a path which climbs away out of the Gorge to Papingo. Low down, from under a sheer rock face, the river reappears full force to go rushing and gurgling downstream. Where they stood, dry river bed, beyond them - a Born Again River! And the water is the blue of heaven, pure, clear, crystalline.

From there they climbed and climbed, a weary trek, but the view out of the Gorge across to the mountain of Nemertsika in Albania was breathtaking, and the view back the way they had come, of crags silhouetted against mist lit to a shiny brilliance by the afternoon sun, was nothing short of miraculous. Gradually rounding the buttress of The Towers they came at last to woodland and a pretty track with mossed and rocky verges harbouring all kinds of plantlife. Stunted juniper and small leafed maple, the result of years of over grazing, create a dwarfish landscape for a while, but then the path moves away up another hillside and they climbed slowly to the village of Mikro Papingo. Past a crumbling stone wellhouse, down an overgrown cobbled street and round a corner they arrived at the hotel where they were to spend the night. By this time their feet were automatons and the first thing they yearned to do was get their boots off. They drank steaming cups of Mountain Tea, brewed from a herb that only grows high up in the mountains and is known for its relaxing and restorative powers. With a spoonful of honey stirred in, it is the walker's elixir.

The following day, the party climbed from Mikro Papingo to the Mountain Refuge where they were going to spend their next night. It sits on a shoulder of land way above the tree line, linking the mass of Astraka on the right with Lapatos on the left. Beyond the shoulder, which drops as steeply on the far side as on the ascent side, rises the peak of Gamila on the crest of which lies the fantastic Dragon Lake. This was their ultimate destination that day.

After installing themselves in the Refuge and lunching, it was quite late in the afternoon when they set out and, with it being November and the days drawing in, the sun was dropping below the skyline by the time they reached the Lake. It sits, incredibly, in a cup of land on the uppermost rim of the mountain, a smooth sheet of water amongst long, pale, reed-like grass. Behind is a short, steep hillside and from the edge of that a sheer and frightening drop. The view of range after range of peaks fading into the blue beyond, makes you aware how much of Greece's landmass is inaccessible and uninhabitable. They watched the sun set on the water of the Lake before making the return journey, the skyline blackening dramatically against the pale, sun drained sky. Night fell and they were amazed how, long after it was dark, the stones along the way seemed to retain a white radiance of their own. There was no presence of fear, such as you might expect alone in that deserted wasteland, but a great sense of peace and the feeling that with the setting of the sun the purpose of the day had been fulfilled.

From the Refuge, the next day, they walked twelve kilometres through the moonscape of the Plain of Gamila, with ravens wheeling overhead and white, wind drawn patterns of cloud against a china blue sky. Their destination was Tsepelovo, where they met Alex Gouris, staying in his pension and dining that night excellently well in his cosy little taverna in the village square.

Finally they climbed, a stiff start to a day's walking, out of Tsepelovo heading for Vradhetto, the highest village in Zagoria, a mile or so in from the edge of the Gorge on the opposite side to Monodendri. There is now a road of sorts to Vradhetto but originally the only access to the village was a paved and walled, stepped muletrack which zigzags in unbelievable fashion up a sheer steep gulley. It was down this stepped track that they descended before picking up the old road to Koukouli. From Koukouli, after a short spell on the main road which, with there being so very little traffic was no hardship, they descended into the shallower upper reaches of the Gorge. Over a soaring, single arched bridge and up steps that lead to the village of Vitsa, after another hour and a half they were back in Monodendri. They had come full circle.

Since this, their first trek together in Zagoria, Ann and Effie have joined several groups and always come back elevated and enthralled, with tales of bear prints frozen overnight into mud, wolf tracks around lakes, golden eagles, carpets of gentians and once, a chamois on a high ridge standing like a stag at bay. On several occasions, setting out from Tsepelovo, they have been joined by a shaggy black dog who happily walks the fourteen kilometres to Monodendri. The only thing that worries her is if a member of the group lingers or gets ahead, and then she anxiously runs to and fro, shepherding them back into line. When the group reaches their destination they have to telephone Alex Gouris to alert her owners so they know to come and pick her up, but she's always most reluctant to leave her flock behind.

With summer well on its way it became important for us to arrange for the construction of a water sterna if we were to avoid the kind of shortages we incurred on our arrival. Mitsos, who was at work in nearby Ano Pedina, came over one evening to discuss the project. On Corfu, our sole source of water had been a ten cubic metre metal tank, above ground, which was refilled by lorry whenever it ran out. There we had a large garden and with the intense summer heat the flowers needed perpetual watering. We also had a small swimming pool which occasionally needed topping up. One tank load of water could be made to last two months, and in Koukouli, not having the same water guzzling luxuries, we reckoned that a sterna of about the same size would see us through any emergency. The thing was, where should we put it? Down by the gate was ruled out. Mitsos decreed that it would weaken the foundations of both houses. We wandered round to the back garden.

"How big do you want it?" he asked and being told, paced out the measurements. After some thought, and a couple of cigarettes, he told us his conclusions.

"This is definitely the best place. The mains water comes down the lane and into your sterna, right? Whilst you have mains pressure you'll be able to gravity feed from the sterna to the house and when the pressure is low all you need is a small pump to boost it. Simple!"

He smiled his engaging smile and Effie purred. Then he began pacing again.

"Ten cubics is O.K." he said. "But whilst I've got the bobcat here, we might just as well make it twenty and then you'll have plenty of water."

It would cost a bit more of course, but then if we found out that ten was not enough it would be an awful bore to have to dig another sterna and probably twice as expensive. And if we succeeded in getting our plan for running a small hotel off the ground, then it made a lot more sense. We agreed, and over a drink Mitsos did his calculations and a price was settled upon. He would begin work the following week.

They start work early in Greece, and the unsilenced bobcat jangling its way up the village streets penetrated our consciousness, bringing us out of bed with a jolt. Flinging on clothes we managed to look the picture of composure as we greeted Mitsos at the gate just after seven in the morning! One of his workmates we knew, he was a stonemason who had worked on our house, the other, a tall wiry man, was Mitsos' tame Albanian. The bulldozer unleashed its hungry jaws and within a few hours there was a cavernous hole in the ground and a disproportionately huge mountain of earth to one side. The two men were down in the pit shovelling out what the dozer couldn't nibble. Seemingly still hungry, it scooped a great mouthful from the mountain and trundled off down the lane to dump it over the edge of the road down the hillside. Several journeys later the pile had all gone, and by the end of the day we had a great, gaping hole... and it began to rain!

It rained solidly for the next two days; however, as

soon as it faired up Mitsos was back with sand, cement, shuttering, reinforcing mesh and a cement mixer, all brought up by the bobcat a great deal more speedily than we could have done with Suzi. The treads chewed into our rain sodden garden turning it into a mud bath, but in five working days the sterna was finished, complete with metal inspection hatch. Mitsos went back to his job in Ano Pedina, assuring us that it wouldn't leak.

Our swimming pool experience in Corfu had taught us that this was not always the case with cemented holes in the ground and to play safe we bought some special, non-toxic sealant to paint over the inside surfaces of the walls and floor. Down in the hot, humid depths of the sterna we sweated away with this dripping solution, working gradually side by side towards the hatch until the only place left was up and out. Our original stocky plumber arrived with the pump, piping and all the tools of his trade. He was a man in a perpetual hurry. So swift and accurate were his actions that he didn't even bother to turn off the mains to join us up. There was just a short jet of water, unwittingly aimed at me, and it was done. He installed the pump, twiddled with a few tuning screws and was off down the lane like a doctor anxious to get to his next case.

The exciting part now was to get the sterna filled before the summer people arrived! This had to be done with a certain amount of surreptitiousness since the village sterna's overflow had stopped, and all of us were relying on the spring to keep topping up the level on a day to day basis. We had no wish to be hanged, drawn and quartered for taking all the village water supply in one go. Probably to prevent just such pirating of water, it is impossible to get a hose attachment that will fit onto a domestic tap and I wrestled for hours making a modification to an old fitment so it wouldn't, under pressure, break away and flood the kitchen. The hose pipe we took up the stairs, through the bedroom, and out through the study window into the sterna so that no-one could see what was going on. This rigged up, we planned to give it a two hour blast a day until it was filled. I measured our first day's catch with alarm! At this rate the summer people would have been and gone before the sterna was full. It was obvious we would have to increase the hours.

In the course of this programme I met Petros in the square. He stood with his hands behind his back like an interrogating schoolmaster.

"How's your sterna?"

"Very good," I replied, ambiguously.

"Filling it, are you?"

"Yes but only an hour a day," I lied.

"Why only an hour?"

"Well, I don't want to take all the water at once."

"Why not?"

"I thought it would be a bit unfair on the summer people."

"Unfair?!" he spluttered, excitably. "Don't you worry about them! You live here all the year round. There's plenty of water. You fill your sterna, keep the pipe running until it's..." He waved his hand high above his head to indicate 'to the top' and shuffled off, kicking a stone out of his path as he went.

To be sanctioned by Petros to do what we knew we needed to do was wonderful news and we ran the hose for the next three days until the sterna was well and truly full. A week later, the first of the summer people moved in.

*

Papa Kostas was doing some major structural work on a house at the back of the village belonging to Petros' two brothers. The roof had to be replaced as the old timbers were rotten, and shifting the stones from one part to another whilst the new timbers were installed was hard work; even harder when done single-handedly.

One evening a young, tall, fair haired Albanian, typical pillowcase slung over his shoulder, wandered into Koukouli and stopped at one of the springs by the church for a wash and a drink. Papa Kostas and I were sitting on the wall in the square and watched him. He had an unhurried, unpersecuted air about him and was slightly better dressed than the Albanians we had seen before, although he'd obviously been on the road. Not a bit abashed at being scrutinised, he came over and sat on the wall with us, carefully putting his sack on the ground between his feet. I offered him a cigarette which he courteously refused. Papa Kostas asked him where he was headed for.

"Wherever there's work."

"What's your name?" he asked.

"David."

We introduced ourselves and sat there with David, chatting. Papa Kostas had become very wary of engaging Albanians to help him, partly because they were such a cheerless lot to work with but also because, after years of communist domination, they were incapable of thinking for themselves, and it became wearisome and time-wasting for him to be constantly breaking off to tell them what to do and how. But he obviously liked the cut of David because, after a short silence, he suddenly said, "Have you had anything to eat?"

"Not for a while."

He stood up and motioned for us both to follow him to his house.

Sitting outside in the courtyard Elevtheria, on instruction from Papa Kostas, brought out bread, feta, olives, a plate of meatballs and a beer for David. We could see that he was starvingly hungry but with a certain dignity he held back and didn't rush the food. When he'd finished eating, he thanked Elevtheria, stacked the plates, poured some beer and relaxed in his chair.

He came from a small township in northern Epirus, just across the straights from Corfu. He'd left his wife with a baby at home telling her he would be back at the end of the summer; taken a bus as close as he could to the border and been walking for the last ten days. He wanted work to earn valuable drachmas to take back to his family. Kostas by this time had decided that here was just the pair of hands he needed and then and there David was taken on. All that remained was to find him somewhere to sleep in the village. The quality of accommodation is not something that over worries the Albanians, and David's temporary home was the small tin shed that the walnuts had landed on that first night we were in Koukouli.

I went up to the house a day later to see how they were getting on. Papa Kostas was obviously delighted with David, with his work, his cheerfulness and sheer sense of fun. The children grew very fond of him and in the evenings, on a flat piece of land near the square, this giant of a man could be seen weaving a football round the panting boys and yelping with delight whenever a goal was scored, be it his or theirs. David was happy and prepared to stay for the summer. Others in the village got to know him and when Papa Kostas had a lull in work would usually find something he could be paid to do. As an Albanian he was such a change from the others we had experienced, and honest to a fault. He would fill up empty plastic bottles with water and every evening, in the privacy of his shed, wash thoroughly, even laundering his few clothes regularly at the springs. To save him traipsing to the church every time he needed water we told him he could take it from our outside tap by the gate, there was no need to ask. Despite that he always did ask, and always thanked us.

They had nearly finished the roof when, looking down one day to the street below, both of them in working clothes and covered in dust, they saw four smartly dressed people, the men in designer casuals and the women in fashionable leather jackets with vastly padded shoulders, wearing what appeared to be a portable jewellery shop on each hand.

"Athenians!" whispered Papa Kostas to David.

Without introduction, one fat, mauve lipped gargoyle shouted up, "Where's the Papas? We want the key to see inside the church!"

"The Papas?" said Kostas, slowly, as if in thought. "The Papas has gone to Ioannina and won't be back until tomorrow."

"Then who else has the key?"

"No-one but God," Papa Kostas replied, turning with a devilish grin to get on with his work.

There were new noises in Koukouli, new voices calling across the village throughout the day. Silent houses slowly came to life as the absentee villagers returned to take advantage of the relative coolness of Zagoria. This was their refuge from the stifling polluted heat of Athens or the blistering dryness of the plains. The arrival routine was much the same from one household to another. Windows and shutters were thrown open to let out stale winter air and let in the warming sunshine. Sheets and bedding were draped over balconies and railings, brooms and buckets of precious water sluiced clean the floors and courtyards. Bedraggled gardens and vines welcomed the gentle attention given them after a winter of neglect and within a few days the houses and their owners settled into a pattern of residence.

Kleoniki was our summer neighbour, arriving in June with her daughter and son in law from Arta. Her house was so old, not even the stonemason's carved plaque offered a clue to its age. Widowed fifteen years, she lives in Koukouli for the most part on her own and became, for us, a continual source of fascination. She is one of those women who seem to feel their honour is at stake if they stop cleaning even for one moment. On her arrival we quite understood that the house would have to be cleaned and aired, the same as everybody else's, but after a week she was still at it. She was still at it the following week and still at it when she left at the end of the summer.

It was an astonishing performance. The great bulk of the day was spent mopping, washing, sluicing down, cooking, shaking mattresses out of windows, sweeping, scrubbing and generally kicking up a rumpus. In the evenings, provided a leaf hadn't landed in her courtyard to be immediately scooped up, she would sit, bespectacled, quietly executing metre after metre of exquisite crocheting. Slightly cantankerous she could be as stubborn as an ox. One weekend, her daughter, son in law and teenage grandchildren came to visit. They had brought with them a number of boxes of tiles for the new bathroom she was having built. The boys were carrying the boxes up the lane one by one when Kleoniki came staggering up with TWO boxes skilfully roped to her back, like a donkey, sweating and puffing. Pointless to ask why, at over seventy, she didn't leave it to the rest of the family. No, she was just that type of woman - couldn't have lived with herself if she hadn't turned it into a personal endurance test.

Early next morning, the minute her weekend visitors had left, the cleaning began obsessively and two days of frantic activity followed before she settled into her normal, time consuming routine.

We also noticed, a little way down the lane, a retired couple who spent almost every weekend in their house and who obviously came from the same school of thought. Winter and summer alike, once in residence their ritual began and went on until the moment they left. The wire netting round their courtyard walls was festooned with rugs and blankets, tin pails clanked and clattered and the lane ran with sudsy water as flagged floors and courtyards were sluiced copiously. Considering the house was shut up during the week, and this cleaning occurred every time they came, we could only think the dust was imaginary. When Kleoniki and Pelagia were together in the village, the competition between the two houses as to who could keep it up the longest reached fever pitch. Way after dark we could still hear pails being filled, rugs shaken, or something, somewhere, being brutally swept.

Petros and Maria, with the influx of summer people, reopened the kafeneon in the square, the central meeting place for gossip to be caught up on, rumours to be circulated and enquiries made into the health of elders and the progress of youngsters. In the evenings the square fills slowly, firstly with the men drifting in from their day's occupations followed by the shepherds a little later when the flocks have been milked and corralled. Over chipero and beers they talk politics and spiralling prices, sheep management and pastures. In a corner two men slam the dice in a game of backgammon. In another, cards are thrown onto the table with loud "Pahh's!" at a winning hand. The women, who come down to the springs with jugs for their drinking water, stop for a while to chat to a friend or cousin before returning home. Sometimes, but very rarely, one of the men gets amicably drunk and becomes the butt of a series of harmless jokes, the others recognising a not-to-be-missed source of entertainment. Lovely, lingering summer evenings under the cool umbrella of the plane tree are spent at the kafeneon, which plays such an important part in the fabric of village life into which, happily, we are becoming accepted as an integral part.

Visitors to Koukouli

The bell rang at the gate door, and opening it I was confronted by two middle aged strangers with a small, West Highland terrier on a lead. The man spoke,

"Ah! So! You are the Englishman we were told to come and see. Very good."

There was a trace of an accent which I guessed correctly to be Dutch. They introduced themselves and their dog, Buddy, who was interestedly inspecting my ankles as a possible place to cock his leg.

Bart and Lian were touring Zagoria for the first time and like us had fallen in love with it. Bart was a freelance company Trouble-Shooter, still taking on occasional assignments if it suited him, but for the most part retired. He and Lian had a house in Paxos, the small island five miles to the south of Corfu, once a delightfully uncrowded place, serviced by a battered unseaworthy ferry that had a permanent list to port and could only take three cars on board at a time. This rusty hulk had unwittingly played an important part in ensuring Paxos remained relatively free of cars and people. However progress, if that's the right word, has recently spawned two passenger ferries continually plying back and forth from Corfu and worse still, a large car ferry direct to Paxos from Italy. This latter brings thousands of Italians and their cars to recreate on Paxos miniature Italian traffic jams. It is now almost impossible to motor anywhere on the island during the summer and the beaches are crowded with people and speedboats and all the noise and unpleasantness that unbridled crowds of holidaymakers bring.

For this reason Bart and Lian were looking for somewhere they could escape to when the hordes moved in. They were interested in our story of coming to Zagoria and wondered about the possibility of finding a house for themselves in the area. We hadn't heard of any for sale but gave them Eleni's phone number; we felt sure she would know if there was anything on the market.

It transpired that she did and after several months of to-ing and fro-ing Bart and Lian succeeded in buying a couple of stone barns in an orchard on the outskirts of Kipi with a marvellous view down to the three-arched bridge. By this time we had got to know them quite well, and on the day they signed their contract we went together for a celebration lunch to the taverna in Dilofo.

The plateia in Dilofo is very spacious, with the taverna at the back of the square dominated by the usual massively spreading plane tree, under which twenty tables with multi-coloured cloths were arranged, each with a jam jar of wild flowers in the centre. Bart and Lian were in high spirits, plans for the conversion of their barns already churning through their minds and we, in turn, delighted at the prospect of having such companionable neighbours.

The landlord came out to take our order, a short stocky man with a suspiciously set smile, darting inquisitive eyes and dirty finger nails, wearing a long white butcher's apron which came down to his shoes. Champagne was not available so we settled for a bottle of semi-sparkling Zitsa wine and a mezedes of nibbles while he prepared our main courses. The food was all excellent and, with more wine and the square to ourselves, our party relaxed into a happy haze amid an idyllic setting. A donkey tethered in the shade of an arched wellhouse quietly dozed, head hanging. Chicken pecked along the side streets, a woman ushered a handful of sheep through the square, bees droned amongst the flowers on the table, and Buddy slept soundly, his lead securely tied to Bart's chair leg.

The time came to leave and we asked for the bill. Lian wandered off to study the shapes of the leaves on the plane tree while Bart and I went into the taverna to pay. Buddy, it turned out, far from being asleep under Bart's chair, had spent most of the time eyeing the passing chicken with gimlet eyes. His lead was of the retractable, extendable type and as Effie bent to untie it, the plastic handle was pulled from her hand and Buddy was off like a rocket! He darted in a straight line between the maze of tables and chairs with the lead streaming behind him, the plastic handle crashing and banging into the objects he so amazingly avoided. The chicken scattered squawking and ran ponderously in all directions as Buddy bore through them having already selected his target. Lian abandoned her botanical pursuits and shot off after him, followed by Effie. The landlord's overweight wife came in a miserable fourth. The outright winner, no need for an action replay, was Buddy, and he accomplished the ambition his tiny strategic mind had been working on all through our long, leisurely lunch. The chicken was dead within seconds of his assault and he was rapturously proud of his first ever kill.

The landlord's wife, with the victim in her arms, its neck dangling with droplets of blood, was not so impressed. She disappeared into the kitchen with the corpse. The leery smile of the landlord had completely vanished. Listening to our profuse apologies he stood as if carved out of stone, his darting eyes fixed now in a trauma of rage. Through clenched teeth he demanded 2000 drachmas for the chicken which we handed over to him without recourse to barter. Thanking the wife for a superb meal we walked away leaving the landlord still rooted to the ground, rigid as a totem pole.

The irrepressible Buddy was being scolded to no effect. His little tail wagged in a blur of circles from sheer delight over what would, otherwise, have been a deadly boring afternoon for him. The humorous side of the event was beginning to catch up with us when, halfway back to the car, Effie's Yorkshire instincts stopped us in our tracks.

"Just a minute," she exclaimed. "We've paid 2000 drachmas for that bird and I bet tonight it'll be put in the pot and served up to some unsuspecting customer for another 2000! No way. I'm going back. That chicken's OURS!"

The rest of us elected to stay behind, thinking that perhaps we had anyway outstayed our welcome and our return, en masse, would not exactly help an already embarrassing situation.

Upon re-entering the plateia, Effie was confronted with the extraordinary sight of the landlord, in his long white apron, kicking over everything in the square with Kung-Fu Kicks! Like a demented dwarf he was lashing out at tables, chairs, dogs, or anything else that happened to be in his path. His language, though indecipherable above the noise he was making, was recognisably blasphemous. Catching sight of her approach, he slowed down in mid kick, dissolved into the pretence of practising some complicated Greek Dance step and danced his way out of sight round the back of the taverna. Effie explained to his wife the reason for her return and with total calm, as if her husband's actions were an everyday affair, she put the chicken into a plastic bag and handed it over. So, now we had a moral victory and a chicken we didn't know what to do with, none of us having any experience of plucking a freshly dead fowl. Bart finally solved the problem by electing to take the chicken back with him to Eleni's hotel, where they were staying, and handing it over to the chef!

Throughout our first summer we met an amazing amount of people from outside the village. Tourism, for Greeks within their own country, is a relatively new pursuit. Most people living in big cities such as Athens are accustomed to spending any free time returning to their home villages. But with the improvement of living standards, and cash to spare, they are beginning to discover and explore the delights and treasures of their own country. The uniqueness of Zagoria has been portrayed in several documentaries shown on Greek Television and this has helped open the eyes of city-bound Greeks to the area.

The villagers in Koukouli took it upon themselves to assume that any non-Greek tourists discovered wandering around the village must be looking for us, and whether they liked it or not they were delivered to our door like trophies. Occasionally, I have to confess, our captive guests turned out to have come to view the house and us as you would a caged animal in a zoo. But for the most part we met delightfully entertaining people with a genuine interest in the history of Zagoria and what we were doing here. Our Visitors Book, given as a Christmas present and intended for use in the hotel, is already half filled with names and addresses from all over the globe. This input of people, the exchange of ideas with people from different backgrounds and nationalities is something we did not expect to find when first we came to Koukouli. Then we had had to agree with sceptical friends that we were probably going to be living in an intellectual vacuum, but it turned out not to be the case at all.

On one occasion we had driven out for the day to Mikro Papingo and after lunch had stopped at an enchanting place where a small rivulet cascades for over half a mile through a series of softly sculptured pools. The water is ice cold from the melted snow on the mountains and swimming in one of the pools is limited to thirty seconds for a coward like me, and thirty five for a hero. Two other English people happened to be there, sitting on the rocks quietly reading, and we naturally fell into conversation with them.

This was their first visit to Zagoria, although they were familiar with other parts of Greece, and by all accounts they fully intended to make it a regular part of future holidays. Andrew was a priest in the Church of England, or as he called it a priest/manager, with seven churches in the Cotswolds under his care. The Church, like any other concern in times of recession, was having to cut back to make ends meet. During his theological training Andrew had made a long study of the workings of the Greek Orthodox Church and was very interested in the fact that most rural priests in Greece have a second job. He was trying to evolve a new system for his diocese that would allow each village to elect a resident to be trained to conduct the simpler, everyday services, so that they could be held on a regular basis. Andrew would still conduct the more important christenings, weddings and special services but he felt that this scheme would enable the churches to function very much more as an integral part of village life, not just on a "Third Sunday in the month? It must be us" basis. His thinking coincided very much with our own observations concerning the life of the church in Koukouli, so we invited him and his wife Susan to the village the following day, to meet Papa Kostas.

Normally I never think to ask Kostas to open the church for visitors or friends because the villagers' faith is a very personal part of their lives and the church, symbolic of that belief, is not there to be gawked at merely for its architectural qualities. On this occasion I did ask because I could see that Andrew and Susan would admire it with a real appreciation of what it was and stood for, and Papa Kostas consented.

With us all sitting round their kitchen table, Elevtheria and all the children somehow squeezed in as well, Andrew and Papa Kostas exchanged views, and ecclesiastical books of saints and Greek Orthodox clergy were brought out and poured over. Andrew spoke clear, slow Greek and where he couldn't follow Papa Kostas, Kiki translated feeling very important. After nearly an hour of animated discussion, we left for the church. Inside, Andrew stopped in amazement and stood, just as we had the first time, awestruck by its magnificence and sheer 'presence'. Recalling himself, he made formal obeisance toward the altar before setting off on a tour. He was astonished at the quality of the wall paintings, explaining to us that as a general rule they followed a similar pattern throughout the Orthodox churches of this era, but here were a series he had never encountered before. Delighted by Andrew's knowledgeable response, Papa Kostas led him round, pointing out certain aspects of particular interest and explaining a little of their history. The central chandelier, for instance, was a gift to the church from the father of a girl, diagnosed as dumb, who as recently as 1981 had miraculously begun to speak upon entering the church.

Finally Andrew turned to Kiki and asked if it would be possible for him to offer a prayer together with Papa Kostas. As Kiki translated this request there was a slightly apprehensive look in Kostas' eyes.

"The prayer would have to be from the Greek Orthodox Service and spoken in ancient Greek," he replied, doubtfully.

"Of course," said Andrew. "I speak and read ancient Greek; it's just Modern Greek I have difficulty with."

They both retreated behind the iconostasis and, in front of the altar upon which Papa Kostas had laid the book of words, they stood together and softly intoned their prayer. It was a strangely moving moment in those surroundings, Andrew in holiday casuals and Papa Kostas, his shirt hanging out over working jeans, toothpick behind his ear, with the dust motes shimmering through a beam of sun from the window above them. In all probability the first time in Koukouli Church that an English priest has joined the Papas in prayer.

Apart from chance meetings with people, as in the case of Andrew and his wife, and the herded tourists from the village, we also had visits from our more adventurous English friends who had come to the conclusion that a holiday split between Corfu and Zagoria would make a change. Since the plans for our hotel were still in their infancy and bogged down with bureaucratic red tape, we put our people up in various other establishments and with this form of Market Research, or Industrial Espionage, we gleaned information on how our future opposition was working. A certain amount of feedback had to be taken with a pinch of salt owing to the language barrier but one thing that amazed us was that nowhere, it seems, could you have a boiled egg for breakfast in an egg cup. Our guests told us, with variations on the story, of incredible juggling acts performed when a scalding egg was delivered, spinning at high speed on a saucer, with no implement to eat it.

Information received on the state of the toilets came as no surprise. The Greeks have not yet moved into the twentieth century where this basic form of technology is concerned and by the side of most lavatories you will find a nasty little pedal bin, usually with brown cigarette burns around the edge of the lid, in which to put used toilet paper and unmentionable objects. Frequently the flush doesn't flush and to have a lavatory seat is the height of luxury even if the rest of the system malfunctions. A plaque that we saw on one of our travels summed up the whole sordid business aptly by clearly stating: Please do not put anything down this toilet that you have not first eaten!

As a result of our research, with the same niggling complaints beginning to repeat themselves, we know now to channel our visitors into the delightful, five roomed, Pension Artemis in Kipi, run by Vangelis Vlakopolou and his wife, Mina. Apart from the fact that the rooms retain many old and intriguing features, we never had any complaints from people we sent there, only compliments on working toilets, availability of hot water, central heating actually switched on, and Vangelis' easy charm and willingness to ensure his clients' comfort and cater to their whims. We have now supplied him with half a dozen egg cups which, we feel, should entitle him to another star from the Greek Tourist Board.

Perhaps it was because we were the only foreign people living in Zagoria all the year round that we were invited into people's homes in other villages. Conversation would normally start innocently enough with the opening lines, "Where do you come from?" and "Where do you live?" A few more exploratory questions bring the dawning realisation that they have heard of us on bush telegraph.

"Oh! Y-O-U-'re the English from Koukouli!"

As a result of one of these encounters with an elderly man outside the kafeneon in Elati, the village opposite us on the northerly face of Mitsikeli, we found ourselves being led down a narrow lane to his house. The usual lychgate opened into a wide and spacious courtyard with a tall house of unusually elegant proportions and beyond, nearly two acres of unwalled land with fruit trees and a couple of outhouses. He introduced us to his wife and together they showed us around.

Although the houses in the Zagorian villages share the same characteristics, being built and roofed in stone, certain influences from abroad have been introduced. In this instance, the elderly man's grandfather had left Zagoria and settled in Vienna where he studied to become a pharmacist. Later, having made his fortune there, he returned to the village and built the house which very definitely bore a strong Viennese influence. The upper floor's louvered shutters and windows were tall and graceful with ornate cast iron balustrading across the lower half. Inside, curtain ties on either side in the walls were made of brass with painted porcelain insets. The sweeping staircase had newel posts topped with faceted balls of ruby glass and downstairs similar touches pervaded. A handsomely framed, tinted photograph of the grandfather hung on the library wall and there was a specially built, mahogany and glass cabinet where all his pharmaceutical test tubes, bottles, phials, scales and other implements were displayed. This lovely house had been inherited by our elderly guide and his three brothers and was used only occasionally as a holiday home. Since none of the other brothers had any interest in spending money to repair or restore it, it was sadly showing signs of decay; walls cracking, ceilings stained where the rain leaked in, rotting window frames and moth eaten furnishings.

There was a house we saw in another village which had French windows opening onto little balustraded balconies; another had a Russian look about it and yet another the grace of a Venetian house. The predominant style is, of course, Zagorian, but seeing these variations moulded into an overall pattern tells something of the history of the people who lived in them. I suppose, in years to come, our house will say something about us and be added to the list of historical oddities.

Agia Paraskevi is a small church belonging to Koukouli, some two miles away, that sits on top of a pinnacle of rock with a sheer drop of 500 feet to the river below. So fantastic are some of the sitings of these isolated churches that we have come to call them "God Spots". At Agia Paraskevi, the annual service held on its Saint's nameday fell on a beautiful clear, sunlit morning with the last of the wild flowers fighting for survival in the summer heat. At half past nine, the villagers gathered to set off in a gaily coloured group down the track from the village. A winding path up a steep and difficult climb failed to deter the older members of the community, although I had serious doubts of my own abilities, and spent five minutes regaining my breath before the final assault. I arrived, panting, into a crowd of nearly a hundred people all jammed together atop the pinnacle, exactly in the manner I always imagined they would when it is announced the end of the world is nigh.

The church was far too small to accommodate this throng who had come from Kipi, Kapesovo and Dilofo as well as Koukouli, and the people sitting and standing about outside resembled a gathering at a summer garden party. Papa Kostas' voice could be heard from within, but lacking the acoustic advantage of his main church. Black- clad grandmothers held babies on their knees, wiped children's noses and handed out sweets. People who obviously hadn't met for a while formed animated groups and a few of the older men, in flat hats and short sleeved shirts, sat on a fallen tree trunk having a forceful political discussion. Children threw stones over the unrailed precipice but nobody seemed to worry, and someone with binoculars was following the flight of a buzzard.

Eventually, the service over, an unbelievable number of people squeezed out of the little church into the open, bumping into acquaintances they hadn't known were there. New groups formed, new conversations were struck up until gradually, everyone began to drift away. Thalia and Aspasia had walked from Koukouli in the morning but now, at noon, out of the shade of the trees, it was extremely hot and they gratefully accepted the offer of a lift back in Suzi.

They told me that, as children, when the time came for them to move on from the school in Koukouli to a more senior one, they had had to leave home every day at six thirty in the morning and walk an hour and a half to the village of Vitsa, and then walk back again in the afternoon. It's hardly surprising that with this early Olympic training combined with visits on foot to outlying churches and gardening on a serious scale, these elderly people are remarkably fit and rarely in need of a doctor.

On my fiftieth birthday, celebrated with a barbecue in the garden, Thalia and Aspasia gave me the usual congratulations, and with glasses raised announced that they looked forward to attending my hundredth birthday party. If I make it, I have no doubt they will be there!

Village Panegyri, Ioannina and the Pasha

With the return of all the summer people, bringing the population up to a staggering sixty, Koukouli was humming. On every corner I would bump into someone going to their allotments, a friend's house, the kafeneon, or rushing to the village phone. In direct contrast to winter when you could walk three times around the village without meeting a single soul. There was also the sound of children, not only Papa Kostas', but others who had been sent to stay with grandparents during the summer holidays, to be joined later by their parents when they took annual leave. Not having children of my own and with a fairly short fuse where other people's 'little darlings' are concerned, I'm quite sure that under current child welfare legislation in Britain, had I been a father, I would long ago have been hauled in merely for the way in which I can scowl at them.

There wasn't a great deal for these children to do in Koukouli to amuse themselves. The two swings in the grassy play area were in the last throes of rust, and the see-saw didn't. An enthusiastic game of basketball on the uneven village pitch would end up with the opponents lost in clouds of dust. The interaction between Papa Kostas' children and the others appeared to be somewhat distant and so, by process of elimination, the visiting children came to call on us in a last ditch attempt to relieve their boredom.

Greek children take absolute priority in the eyes of all adult members of the family and as a result are over-loved, rarely rebuked and seem to be spoiled rotten. A certain recipe, you would say, for introducing a breed of Super Slobs to wreak havoc on the world at large. But I have to admit that here we have not met one child who is not courteous, polite and helpful. I suspect the answer lies in their having such a strong family unit. As the children grow up they learn to respect the unit and, consequently, other people. All the visiting children in Koukouli spoke English, which they were eager to try out on us, and to our shame the older ones about to move on to university spoke better English than can generally be heard on the average High Street in Britain. So, with our new found chums, we spent many an hour talking, playing cards, singing English songs whose words we could barely remember, and preparing the occasional barbecue. Not only did I amaze myself by enjoying it all, I never once felt inclined to produce my award winning scowl.

Every village has its patron saint, and with Koukouli having more than one church and Greek Orthodoxy having a stock of saints that would fill a supermarket, we had three. However, with the large church being the most important, on its name day, which falls on the fifteenth of August, the annual village party or 'panegyri' was held in the plateia. The church service started as normal at eight in the morning, and whilst this was going on a mini bus turned up, from which four men, dressed in what looked like shiny second-hand mobster suits, and all smoking, slowly observed the scene. This was the band. From the back of the van huge speakers were lugged to a corner in the plateia close to the kafeneon. These were followed by an electric organ, coaxials, leads, plugs, amplifiers and, finally the instruments; clarinet, violin, bouzouki, tambourine and guitar. Watching the band put this lot together was like watching five men trying to unravel a knot in a hosepipe but after an hour they were all seated, having adjusted and got rid of horrendous shrieks and squeals of feedback that must have rattled the teeth of the congregation inside the church. Happy at last, though still unable to resist the occasional tweak to their apparatus, they lit up and settled back to await the start of the panegyri.

Trestle tables of unknown vintage were surrounded by an army of bent tubular chairs missing most of the gaudy woven plastic that originally served as a seat, but still acceptable. Acceptable that is for the broader bummed members of the community, the thinner ones imperceptibly sinking through until only their heads appeared above table level. Maria was busy in the kafeneon whilst Petros, with Minas their son, had set up a vast barbecue made out of split oil drums under one of the well arches. Smoke drifting out through the arches made the whole building look like a Chinese dragon breathing fire.

By half past ten the service was over and from the packed church a hundred and more people flocked out into the square and the band, as if woken from a dream, burst into action. The panegyri had started. Trays of chipero, bottles of beer, orangeade and cola were brought out and, judging by the sizzling smoke, food would not be long in following. Petros' brother was book-keeper and sat inside the kafeneon door with a vast sheet of paper covering an entire table keeping score of what had been ordered and by whom. We mingled and chatted with the people we knew and were introduced to those we didn't. Actual conversation was reduced to a shouting match, or even written notes, as the music had been tweaked to Wembley

Rock Concert proportions. This, however, didn't appear to deter the Greeks who, as a nation seem impervious to noise, and they carried on lip reading and nodding to each other as if the band weren't even playing. The drink flowed and eventually souvlakis appeared by the dozen, along with chunks of lamb and glutinous goat. With bread, olives, feta, paper serviettes, plastic cups and the children's ice cream wrappers, the tables and plateia were quickly strewn with debris. The dancers were picking their way through it all, avoiding a gang of unattended toddlers, keeping the whole thing going; but by two in the afternoon, the majority had retired home for their siesta, leaving the band playing on.

The system with these local bands, so we discovered, is that the first few tunes are financed by the person who engages them, in this case our village mayor. Thereafter, each song is sponsored by individuals for the sum of 1000 drachmas who request whatever they wish to be played. It became apparent to us that people, in their initial enthusiasm, must have inundated the musicians with requests and drachmas because, apart from one hour's break around six in the afternoon, they played on and on and on! Some siesta!

The party rekindled at seven and the plateia was soon jammed. New lights, recently installed in the plane tree, shone brightly down onto a ring of thirty or more dancers, moving rhythmically anti-clockwise, simultaneously swaying.

"Look, look! My father's going to dance!" cried Kiki with a fond mixture of excitement and pride, and sure enough there was Papa Kostas striding out into the square to lead the dance, white handkerchief in his left hand by which the next in line would hold and support him. The music struck up and they were away again. Hatless, Papa

Kostas' face beamed moonlike in the light against the rich darkness of his curling hair and beard, his right arm gracefully carving arcs in the air, feet nimbly kicking the hem of his cassock. Down on his heels he dipped and spun, then up again, back into step and on to another complicated figure. It was obvious he was no mean dancer. Dancing their traditional dances is far and away the favourite pastime with Greeks, and the crowd showed their delight and appreciation at having a Papas who could and did join in and acquitted himself with such panache.

Round and round they went, circling upon themselves as more and more people joined ranks, until over a hundred people were moving perfectly in step. Except that is for one who, with her arms around Kiki and some unknown young man, was desperately trying to keep up. Only towards the end of the evening did Effie manage to get the hang of it and perform the steps as lightly and fluidly as the rest. Alas, it was a short lived achievement - by next day she'd completely forgotten the sequence.

At three in the morning, tired, happy and slightly the worse for wear, we went home and fell into bed, the village still echoing to the glass shattering sound of the band. At six o'clock we were rudely woken by the strident chant of "R-O-Yeee! Oh R-O-Y- eeeeeee!" from a fractured chorus of happy young people in the street outside, simultaneously singing a slurred and unrecognisable song. Naked and bleary eyed I tottered to the upstairs window, threw a five hundred drachma note out into the air, as is the custom with street singers, and staggered back to bed. At that moment the band stopped. Peace reigned at last. We slept until eleven and the village, usually well under way by that time, was silent as a grave. Downstairs in the courtyard, pinned down by a stone, was my five hundred drachma note.

Careful selection of patron saints for the villages in Zagoria means that somewhere there is a panegyri or, as we came to call them after our experience of the one in Koukouli, a 'pain-in-the-eari', practically every day for almost a month. A couple of days after ours, Papa Kostas and the family told us to come up to the one in Kapesovo, the village above ours. We knew the village and the church in the central square and dutifully arrived at nine thirty in the morning to find the church locked, the village deserted and no sign of bands with electronic aids. Even the dogs were missing. We confirmed with each other that we had the right village and the right day. Still nothing happened. On the way back to the car, feeling confused and a little dispirited, we heard faint strains of music and away, far up a hillside, we could make out specks of people being led down from a hilltop church by the band. Not for the first time we'd arrived at the wrong church!

We watched the musicians, like so many pied pipers, leading the congregation back into the village, playing all the way, Papa Kostas in his billowing cassock, stove pipe hat and jutting beard to the fore. Joining the troop and their troubadours we paraded through Kapesovo visiting, one after another, three houses where the families had sons rejoicing in the same name as their patron saint, Ilias. In each, drinks and refreshments were offered to every comer, the band installed themselves and played, the Papas delivered his blessing and on we all trooped to the next, ending up as usual in the village square.

After half an hour of general shuffling about, the musicians got themselves seated and provided with beer, and as people drifted in the day's entertainment got under way. It was the same band we'd had in Koukouli but this time, much to our relief, there were no loudspeakers and the music was far more enjoyable. Here the dancing was predominated by the menfolk, dancing several forms together with great gusto and some alarming gymnastics. One such dance involved a shallow, beaten copper tray filled with water, into which the principal dancer put his socks. Deprived of shoes and with his trouser legs rolled up, he performed the steps of the dance in the tray on top of his socks. Around him the young men twirled and postured, mocking him most amicably with quite explicitly sexual overtones, and a great deal of tomfoolery with extra jugs of water took place. We really wished we could understand the words to the music so we had some clue as to the origins of this strange performance. Finally they took away the tray and his sopping socks and left him with three small glasses, upturned on the ground, on which he danced, barefoot, a most intricate arrangement of moves often for long pauses balancing on the ball of one foot without touching ground. It ended in a frenzy of congratulations as the musicians added an encore of their own for the sheer virtuosity of the dancer.

On yet another occasion, Papa Kostas, entertaining a houseful of friends, sent Kiki up to ask if we could help them with transport problems. Just to go, they said, for half an hour to another village to look at a house. Wanting an early night, but being either stupid or gullible, I eventually agreed.

"But ONLY for half an hour," I pleaded.

"Of course, no more," Papa Kostas replied, all childlike innocence.

Parking the car, we heard the music. "Oh no!" I thought. "Not another panegyri!"

On entering the square seething with people, the band, the kafeneon, the drinks, the familiar faces, Kostas squeezed my shoulder and gave me a huge wink. We had been conned, well and truly conned. Our early night didn't materialise until four in the morning.

Ioannina, the capital of Epirus, is our only shopping centre, an hour's drive along practically empty roads. It is a city of about 130,000 people, with a military base, a large flourishing university and university hospital; a thriving modern city, but with the old quarters around the ancient fortifications still more or less intact. The outstanding feature of Ioannina is undoubtedly Lake Pamvotis, five miles long and some three miles wide, along whose western shore Ioannina lies, looking across to the Mitsikeli range of mountains rising from the opposite shoreline. Much of the charm of Ioannina would be lost without this magnificent stretch of water with the high walled old town, its mosques and minarets, close by the shore's edge. A mile long avenue of plane trees by the lakeside is a popular place to relax, with tavernas, restaurants, cafes, and street vendors hawking popcorn, freshly roasted corn on the cob, nuts, and an array of sticky sweets from hand pulled carts with gaily flapping awnings.

From here you can best see the island in the middle of the lake, wafting with trees, reed bordered, to which flat bottomed bus-boats ferry. Hidden from view on the far side of the island is a small, historical village settlement, preserved for the nation with strict building controls. A twisting, cobble-laned village of white painted stones, shady squares and water's edge restaurants, it boasts five monasteries, guardians of valuable historical and religious documents. The best known, behind the village close by the lake shore, is St. Panteleimon. Steps from the church lead up to three cells above arched storerooms and it was here Ali Pasha fled, at the end of his long despotic rule, and was assassinated. The building, carefully preserved, houses many of his personal effects; costumes of the day and prints of old Ioannina and of principal personages of the time are on display. Some years ago, in a freak gale, a vast limb from one of the towering plane trees behind the museum tore away and crashed onto the building reducing parts of it to rubble. Immediately the Ioanninans took steps to save the historic artefacts, seal off the damage and start restoration. Visiting it now you would be unaware that it was not all original, except that the great plane trees, for obvious reasons, have been lopped, and the building has lost the slightly sinister feeling that the darkness of drooping foliage all around gave it.

In the modern centre of Ioannina there are supermarkets and all the chain store shops with internationally known names to be found in any comparable European city. The more recent architecture has tended to be of the concrete box type in the form of layers of flats and offices over shops but through the centre runs a broad, open boulevard and park, and in all parts of the town you can find verdant, shady squares in which to while away hot summer days. It is encouraging to see that a tighter control is being brought to bear on new construction which must now have a much stronger regard for the past of the city. The new National Bank of Greece is an excellent example of a perfectly modern building in the style of days gone by. Restoration rather than demolition of old buildings is being encouraged, and greater care is being exercised by the authorities to bring back some of the past glory of Ioannina to blend in with the modern. Recently, a huge programme has taken place for the installation of an updated drainage system and at the same time pavements have been freshly laid and planted with trees, and decorative pedestrian areas created. The city is clean, well run, properly organised and the envy of many other Greek cities.

Ioannina's history is long and colourful, dating from the 6th century AD. Its importance developed as a trading post between West and East, enjoying prosperity from trade with Russia, the Balkans, Germany, Venice, Malta and Constantinople. Skills such as gunmaking, crafting silver and copper ware, jewellery, tooling leather and many other crafts brought fame and wealth to Ioannina. The city's zenith came with the arrival, under Turkish occupation, of a new governor or Pasha, called Ali Pasha.

Ali Pasha's trademarks were those of cruelty and terrorism. Born in the Albanian town of Tepeleni around 1740, he was the son of the Vice Governor of the town, Veli, called Pasha of the Two Tails. These Pashas were originally appointed by the Sultan's government in Constantinople, but with power in their hands they usually ended up establishing and enlarging their own fiefdoms. As a result, greed and treachery found them fighting amongst themselves. Veli, being of a particularly quarrelsome nature was reported by his enemies to the Sultan who stripped him of office, and he died shortly after. Ali's mother, Khamco, was a violent, ruthless woman, greedy and out for revenge. Her love for Ali and his sister was a driving force and she had an awe inspiring influence on them until her death. It was she who rallied her dead husband's supporters and urged Ali to become a robber and bandit, overthrowing other Pashas and claiming their wealth for his own. So successful was he, with his ever growing army of accomplices, that it was not long before he became the most notorious and feared man in Albania. His luck eventually ran out when the Pasha of Berat who was chief of police in southern Albania and parts of Greece, captured his gang and sentenced them all to be hanged. Ali however was spared, since the Pasha admired him as a fearless fighter and engaged him instead against his own enemies. On the death of the Pasha of Berat, Ali applied for and got all his titles. The way was now clear and over the years, abetted by his power-hungry mother, he overwhelmed other Pashaliks and added them to his domain.

Ioannina was the one big power he did not have in his arsenal, for which he craved. On hearing that the incumbent Pasha was away from town, he forged an Imperial Decree from the Sultan and presented himself as the newly elected Pasha of Ioannina, forcibly restraining his predecessor from re-entering the city. He was, by this time, fifty years old, and he remained the Pasha of the city until his assassination some thirty years later. Although Ali ruled by terror (grilling people alive in a public place after first flaying them was one of his specialities) he was clever, and quickly realised that the artisans of Ioannina could create enormous wealth given incentive and greater opportunities. To achieve this he was obliged to rely upon the Greeks, as the Islamic faith frowned upon any form of commerce amongst its people. So he gave concessions to the Greek, and Jewish, communities within the city allowing them to keep their churches and synagogues and run their own schools, together with other beneficial privileges. He encouraged trade fairs, international bazaars and exhibitions and as his subjects became wealthier he was enabled to extract more taxes from them and so increase his own wealth. His civil service was run by

Epirote Greeks who were renowned for their organisational abilities. Through Ali's administration, Ioannina became the most prosperous city in the entire Balkans and from this base of wealth and power he gradually came to dominate almost the whole of Greece.

Ali Pasha was, by all reports, a smallish, cherubic man with fair hair and blue eyes, imbuing him with an overall appearance of honesty and integrity. He gave court to many foreigners who passed through the city on their travels, including Lord Byron who wrote that he found him "most charming". Indeed, part of Ali's success came from this captivating side of his nature. It was his 'charm' when playing the diplomat that many people tripped up on. There was the occasion when both the French and British were vying for domination of Lefkas in the Ionian Islands, then in French hands. Ali offered to help the British in their attack on the Island, at the same time offering assistance to the French to man their defences, in an attempt to step between them and take Lefkas for himself. His charm, however, failed him in these negotiations and Lefkas never became part of his domain.

On the other hand, Ali was responsible for initiating many public works; the building and improvement of roads and canals, irrigation schemes and the draining of marshlands and, of course, for the mosques and Palace buildings within the fortress. There his officials and staff numbered hundreds, with a strongly disciplined hierarchy. The Palace also boasted a harem of five hundred women to satisfy his seemingly insatiable sex drive and in addition, Ali kept around himself groups of young males in constant attention giving rise to a belief that his greater appetite was homosexual!

THE PAPAS AND THE ENGLISHMAN

By 1820 Ali was nearly eighty years old and through his long and eventful career had, not surprisingly, made many enemies. Those in Constantinople who had access to the ear of the Sultan, eventually persuaded him to depose Ali and his two sons. An Imperial army was despatched to do just that and they advanced upon Ioannina. His sons were lured away by promises of fresh titles in Asia Minor if they deserted their father, and most of Ali's 15,000-strong army went over to the Sultan, leaving him with just a few thousand loyalists. Ali, always invigorated by the thought of a fight, set about destroying the town outside the fortress so that his enemy, upon arrival would find no shelter. A siege ensued. After six months in which Ali somehow managed to hold the fortress, news came to him that far from being given their promised Pashaliks his sons had been beheaded. At the same time, because of his meanness with pay, many remaining soldiers deserted, and any hope of continuing to hold the garrison against the Turks disappeared. Ali himself was worn out.

Kurshid Pasha, the General in charge of the Imperial Army, saw his opportunity and sent messages to Ali saying that the Sultan was prepared to give him a pardon and a high position in Constantinople if he would hand over Ioannina. Ali refused: finally, however, he agreed to meet Kurshid Pasha for negotiations at the monastery on the island, and took himself and a few retainers there to wait. Kurshid's officers tried to persuade him to hand over the fortress first as a part of his 'Plea Bargaining', but Ali stood firm. Later, after several days left waiting in suspense on the island he changed his mind, and handed his garrison over to the Turks.

That same day, a boat set out from Ioannina to the island. As Ali stepped onto the balcony of the monastic cell to greet his pardon he was met by a hail of bullets. He and every last man with him were killed. His head, proof of his demise, was hacked off and sent to the Sultan; his body was buried in the citadel of Ioannina.

So much wealth had been created by Ali that Ioannina did not decline after his death. He, unlike other Pashas of the day, had developed a strong and lasting infrastructure, and many Epirote families had not only traded outside the Ottoman Empire but also established themselves in many of the main capitals of Europe. Ali had encouraged this exodus of Greeks, to promote trade, but he had always insisted on one or more members of the family remaining in Ioannina, virtual hostages. The Greeks abroad supported, financially at least, the several Hellenic organisations and schools and because of this the culture and prosperity of Ioannina was maintained through Turkish rule. In 1913, with the ultimate collapse of the Ottoman Empire, Ioannina became once more a part of Greece.

Day trip to Albania

One evening we called at a small hotel in the nearby village of Elati to have a drink with Thomas, the proprietor. Thomas, though Greek, had spent many years in Canada before returning to Zagoria and his command of English is excellent. We complimented him on the hand carved chairs and tables in his attractively appointed dining room, and the carved stools and banquettes in the bar.

"From Ioannina?" we asked.

"No. From the factory in Albania. Actually I need to order more and was thinking of going over next week. Why don't you come with me, take a look?"

So strongly brainwashed were we by the idea that Albania was taboo to all Westerners, more especially to an English couple with European Community passports, it had never occurred to us that we could now go there. Thomas assured us that we were entitled and free to do so. He had already been, several times, on his Canadian passport.

The day we drove to Kakavia, the border checkpoint, it was grey, misty and raining. For no reason whatsoever we had imagined that Kakavia would be some sort of township, but we were mistaken. After just under an hour's drive, towards the top of a ridge we drew up onto an open concrete area, wet and slimy with mud, cordoned off into sections with grey tubular railings; bleak, colourless and haunted by spiritless groups of dismal looking people with bags, parcels, and cardboard boxes tied with string, heaped around their feet. Thomas's plan was to park his car here, go across on foot and hope for a taxi on the other side. He dare not risk taking the car into Albania to leave it parked outside the factory. In ten minutes it would have been stripped.

The minute we got out we were set upon by a clamorous gang of swart, black-haired urchins, hands outstretched, grabbing, demanding money. Streetwise Thomas did a deal; if the car was undamaged and intact on our return, he would pay them. We walked away in the direction of the Greek conning tower rising above concrete and crital offices, policed by pistol-packing Greek soldiers in camouflage and boots. A knot of Albanians were pushing to get into the Passport Office. A soldier grabbed our passports and leafed through them. We were curtly told to get a form from a box on the wall. Thomas already had his, and we joined the crush. Inside, Thomas's Canadian passport was duly stamped, but we were summarily dismissed. European Community passports no longer needed to be stamped by Greek Customs.

We approached the border gates, massive steel contraptions that swung open letting the huddles of people on both sides filter through. A long queue across no-man's land of incoming lorries and cars meant we had to splash and pick our way between, breathing diesel, until we came to the Albanian conning tower and offices. Here a narrow doorway with 'passeporte' in stick-on gold lettering was jammed with men trying to force an entry. We joined the scrum. Once through, we found ourselves wedged up against a formica desk strewn with ledgers and papers, facing three uniformed men on the other side. There was only just room for us between the desk and the door. Our passports were grabbed unceremoniously. The most senior official told us we must pay 1,500 drachmas each, so the money was handed over and with much rummaging a receipt book found. Flimsy sheets of carbon paper were unearthed and a minor colleague was put onto writing out the receipt which he did, referring to our passports and previously written receipts with the concentration and doggedness of a schoolboy doing his homework. We were ordered to go past the desk and wait behind, freeing the way for them to continue stamping the passports of the growing horde of Albanians in the doorway. We were at liberty to take stock of our surroundings.

The office had, at some time, been papered in ribbed wallpaper, brown now with nicotine, white patches of plaster glaring through where pieces had come adrift and been torn off. An old sofa-bed which looked as if it had been rescued from a tip that very morning was pushed against the wall. We were told to sit down, but looking at it preferred to stand even though we felt horribly conspicuous, to the point of actually being made to feel guilty. The room was rank with the smell of unwashed humankind and stale damp clothing. The completed receipt was torn out of the book and the Senior Officer took the chair. Details of our passports were entered into a grimy ledger - who, we wondered, would eventually be looking at or checking that? Then the desk drawer was yanked open and a sheet of what appeared to be badly roneo-ed toilet paper drawn out from amongst the jumbled contents. Onto this our details were yet again meticulously written by hand. We watched, mesmerised, as the officer folded the paper, laid the crease along the edge of the desk and carefully tore the top part off. This he folded into three, firming the creases between finger and thumb and tearing it into separate pieces. Sensing our fascinated gaze he looked up, and by way of explanation uttered the word, "Visas!"

We dared not smile but remained poker faced until all was bundled together and with a wave of the hand we were dismissed out into the drizzling rain.

Our first steps into Albania landed us on an open, mud-rilled hillside, chaotically parked with cars in various stages of collapse. The same dispirited groups of people with their bags, bundles and boxes, lurked between. A man came up and spoke to Thomas. We needed a car? He had a car - follow him. It was a Fiat; a luxury model in its day which must have been many years and thousands of kilometres ago. Inside there was the same damp-clothes smell that was everywhere. Over the headrests on the front seats were two tattered and stained hand towels. A fox's brush, a ceramic heart, crucifix and other talismans hung from the rearview mirror and a plastic advertising sunvisor along the top of the windscreen, peeling at the edges, effectively cut off any view from the back seats. The driver, a Greek speaking Albanian, announced that his name was Vasilis. From behind I could see he hadn't combed his hair that morning; it lay flattened against the back of his head and he suffered from chronic dandruff. He put the keys in the ignition and bent forward to twist together two wires that dangled from the steering wheel. The car leapt about with great clatterings but stubbornly refused to start. At a shout from Vasilis a babble of helpers pushed us backwards and forwards in the mud until we were facing downhill. Gliding away we gradually gained momentum until, with another dreadful shudder the engine reluctantly came into play.

THE PAPAS AND THE ENGLISHMAN

We were off, in an unroadworthy car, with an unknown Epirote driver, into an unknown country along a concrete road, riddled with potholes and frayed at the edge, barely wide enough for two cars. This, the main road into Albania, descended into a vast plain encircled by mountains, their heads in the clouds. Villages materialised on the boulder strewn foothills. The architecture was similar to our villages in Zagoria; stone buildings, well proportioned, with stone slated roofs; but these stood exposed to view, helter-skelter down the hillside without walled courtyards or gateways and no stone-paved streets, just rutted earthen tracks. We never saw a single light on in any of them, though the day was grey and overcast.

The road itself was bordered with poplars on either side but apart from these the entire area seemed devoid of trees. As we progressed through the valley we began to notice how many had been felled, probably to provide householders with fuel. And everywhere, all around, were scattered the concrete humps ten feet across of underground pillboxes, resembling a crop of monstrous mushrooms. Thousands upon thousands of them, gun slits facing towards Greece, imbuing the landscape with an eerie quality of fear.

We passed a few straggling flocks of muddy sheep and an occasional cow or two; saw defunct factories, gravel works, agricultural depots, the buildings abandoned and falling down, black with rust and stained with weather, windows vacant gaping holes with no glass. Wherever a track led off from our road, disconsolate groups of people were gathered with the predictable packages and baggage, sodden in the rain, presumably waiting for a bus. As we went by, dead eyes looked out from dead faces, and some people seemed actively afraid, cowering as we drove past.

We felt as though we were travelling through a country that had just come out of a war.

Thomas wanted to make a detour to visit an Albanian he'd made friends with in Zagoria, so we left the road and set off up a side track running like the road straight as a die, but at right angles to it. On either side were the blackened stumps of felled trees and the menacing pillboxes. Some had been pulled out wholesale, like teeth, leaving great cavities that had filled with brackish water. Bumping up the last few metres to the village we parked, facing downhill, behind a concrete block of flats where two women were washing clothes at an open pipe gushing out of the hillside. The older woman was holding an umbrella over the laundress. Women, children in tow, came with buckets and bottles to fill up with water. Was this open geyser the village's only supply?

Thomas and Vasilis went into a concrete box with an open door which seemed to be the local kafeneon to ask for the friend, and we got out of the car, again feeling uncomfortably conspicuous. A lank-haired man in ragged clothes, trouser bottoms caked in mud, walked out of the open entrance to the flats and stood in the rain, silent, staring, with no facial expression whatsoever. An elderly woman peering out of a broken window patched up with a piece of grubby polythene, flicked aside a grimy rag of a curtain. A small dog yapped, hollowly, from somewhere inside. Thomas's friend had left the village to find work in a town further north so, mission aborted, we climbed into the dampness of the car and bumped off back to the main road.

Finally we approached Argyrokastro the capital city of this southern part of Albania, home of the ethnic Greek minority. On the outskirts like any other town were the industrial areas. Except that here nothing appeared to be working. Everything seemed shut down. Lorries from China, great prehistoric monsters, rotted in factory forecourts. Equally prehistoric farming equipment, not now seen in the West, lay rusting by the roadside. At last we met up with traffic. Uniformed police materialised, whistles in mouth. The driving was scandalous; there were no roadsigns or road markings, no traffic lights, nothing. Thomas guided Vasilis through the town to the woodcarving factory, just off the main street behind a stone tiered sports arena with high black railings and a glimpse on the muddy pitch of an oddly familiar, white goalpost. We clanked to a halt outside a big, tea stained, concrete warehouse with huge factory windows patched with chicken netting and torn polythene. Rainwater poured in streams off the gutterless flat roof. Leaving Vasilis to wait we made a dash for the doorway and entered a pitch black hall from where we could hear the 'tap, tap, tapping' of wooden mallets.

Inside, in two vast interconnected rooms were ranks of old fashioned work benches, each with a worker engaged on a piece of carving; chisels, plastic templates and pencils lying nearby. Chair legs, back sections, panels for chests and caskets, mirror frames, ceiling roses were all being carved to a variety of designs; elk and fir trees, ancient Greek flower symbols, geometric patterns, each painstakingly chipped out of the wood by hand. Alongside, equipped with machinery that in the West would now only see light of day in an industrial museum, was the workshop for cutting and preparing all the variously shaped pieces from raw planks of oak and beech. Without sufficient current to run them they lay idle, their operators gloomily hanging about.

A single flyblown lightbulb dangled overhead; the

workers, a number of them women in stern overalls, perched on high stools bent over their tasks. What daylight there was filtered through filthy, metal framed windows, smothered in a film of damp sawdust and cobweb caught chippings. It was a Dickensian scenario. Government run, there was no question of working conditions conforming to a Factory Act. Though raining, the day was reasonably warm. How would they work in that airhanger when temperatures fell below zero? It didn't bear thinking about.

We wanted something to take back with us, a memento of this extraordinary excursion, and the mirror frames were very beautiful. Did Thomas think we would be allowed to take one back over the border? He did. Well we would like one, carved but without the stain and varnish of the finished article. Sadly, their varnishing technique ended up giving all that exquisite carving the appearance of badly moulded plastic. Wrapped, though with difficulty there being neither string, baling tape nor staple gun available, it was deposited in the car boot. Vasilis had been sitting in the car all this while, smoking, and the windows were completely steamed up.

As soon as we had bump started, we wound them down to get fresh air into our lungs and take a last look at this sadly squalid township with its deserted sports arena, its seamy tenements, most in no better outward condition than the factory; people in the street congregating with nothing to do, the tawdry array of beaten up vans, trucks and Mercedes; shuttered shops, and plastic draped street vendors' stalls hawking unspeakable junk. It was a town with no future, only a painful past and the faces of the men were etched with grim despondency and blank hopelessness.

The rain increased as we drove dismally back to

Kakavia. Having paid Vasilis the 10,000 drachmas he demanded for his services, with our mirror frame very obvious in its flapping wrapping, we walked up to the Albanian Customs. The Senior Official recognised us, took our passports into the office and stamped us back through. He seemed delighted to have us off his books. Tramping across no-man's land and through the barriers once more into Greece we were instantly set upon by the 'guardians of the car', shrieking "Dollars! Dollars!" Thomas paid them in drachmas, thrown across the car park to disperse them, and we made our escape.

At the Greek army post we were stopped. The boot was opened, our passports demanded. Thomas' was passed back but ours posed a problem. The soldier couldn't find our photos and details. He was looking in the front. He leafed his way through empty pages getting more and more embarrassed, and consequently angry, before he came upon the back pages. Whereupon he glowered at us and our pictures and finally thrust them through the window of the car. He was only young, a conscript, cold and wet and bored. Most probably he'd never seen a European Community passport before. How many Europeans would have passed through the checkpoint at Kakavia since the border opened, returning from a day trip to Albania?

The last chapter . . .

Shortly after we had bought the house in Koukouli, on the advice of Eleni our architect, we put in an application for a telephone. It seemed a very odd thing to be doing in the light of our experience of the workings of the Greek Telephone Company, OTE which, at best, is regarded as a National Joke. On Corfu we had asked our landlord about the possibility of getting a phone at Paleomagaza to be told that one had been applied for and OTE had promised to install a line within the year. The year came and went, as did a second one, with no sign of anything being done. At this point I went to the OTE offices to find out exactly what the position was. There, in a dusty ledger, lay the original application, complete with signatures and departmental stamps, dated 22nd March, 1972! The OTE official, sensing my look of astonishment, reassured me that everything possible was being done, that new lines were definitely designated for our area and by Christmas, for sure, we would have a telephone. Now, nine years after my enquiry, Paleomagaza still has no phone and as little likelihood of getting one in the near future as there was, twenty one years ago, when the application was first submitted!

On this basis, we regarded our application here as an optimistic shot in the dark. One day however, coming back from Ioannina, we passed a digger opening up a narrow trench along the side of the road, about ten miles from

Koukouli. We knew it couldn't be either for electricity or water and rounding the bend, to our astonishment, we came upon giant cotton reels of cable being off-loaded onto the verge. Apart from our amazement that work was underway, we were intrigued that they were taking the trouble to lay the cables underground, a very rare thing in Greece outside major cities. Talking to Takis in Kipi, where the central exchange for the new installation was based, we learned that with Zagoria being a National Park it was felt poles or pylons would look ugly and disfiguring. On the face of it, it certainly seemed a serious undertaking. We watched the progress of the digger over the following weeks with fascination; day by day it marched slowly toward Kipi.

Not long afterwards, an advance gang of OTE men in orange helmets arrived in Koukouli, seeking out the houses of people who had applied for a phone. Freshly creosoted poles were placed in strategic positions, just where it was convenient to grab hold of them to take difficult cobbled corners. Black smeared fingermarks on the wall showed where people had tried to rid themselves of the sticky tar. A large junction box materialised, fixed to the side of the kafeneon, and new cables were slung across the village. Excitement was mounting and the OTE activity was followed with plenty of advice from the older men who had nothing better to do, and who were probably incapable themselves of even changing a torch battery.

Petros, armed with fluttering sheaves of paper, came busily round one evening to announce, in his capacity as community officer, that our phone would be installed the next day at ten thirty. In total disbelief we sat down to a stiff chipero.

"Good grief!" I said. "After less than a year living in Koukouli we're going to get our own phone."

"I'll believe it when I see it" muttered Effie. "And since when have the Greeks kept an appointment to such precise timing? Ten thirty indeed!"

At ten thirty on the dot two men from OTE arrived, checked our details, ticked us off their list, had me sign a piece of paper, and left saying they would wire us up from a pole behind the house so we wouldn't have the view from our windows spoiled. Effie was dumbfounded, but she quickly rallied.

"Bet the bloody thing doesn't work!"

Half an hour later the men returned, unboxed a very stylish phone in two-tone grey and plugged it into the jack plug our electrician had seen fit to install when the house was wired up.

Still not defeated, Effie asked, "How many days before we can use it?"

"I'll call you back to test the line."

Fifteen minutes later the phone rang and we both jumped clean out of our skins. Our OTE man confirmed that all was working and we could make calls as from that moment. We were amazed at the speed and efficiency of the whole operation, and two months later equally amazed by the size of our bill.

Even old Vasilia eventually got a phone which she keeps on the windowsill by the window through which she used to shout to Effie. Old habits die hard, and she shouts now down the phone, just as loudly as she always used to and with her window open we receive her in stereo. Before we had these telephones, the villagers used to drop round to each other's houses on the off chance of a chat and a cup of coffee. Now it has all become a bit more formal, with a phone call to arrange specific times in advance. The tannoy in Petros' walnut tree hardly makes a murmur these days. It seems by moving further into the twentieth century a certain native spontaneity has been lost.

The paperwork and planning permits for our projected hotel were still churning through the tunnels of bureaucracy and we had become conditioned to the fact that there was nothing we could do to speed up their progress. It was becoming, however, a matter of gathering urgency to build our planned storeroom and workshop at the back of the house before the onset of winter. Papa Kostas was working on a building in Kapesovo and wouldn't be free for a couple of weeks, which gave us a chance to get all our materials on site. He came round one evening and we paced and pegged the area, and worked out what would be needed in the way of breeze blocks for the internal structure, cement, sand, reinforcing mesh for the floor and timbers for the roof. We telephoned the haulier we'd used before to pick up and deliver everything to Koukouli.

A few days later the first truck load arrived, breeze blocks and bags of cement. By the time we had shifted this lot in Suzi to the back of the garden, the sand had arrived. The last load was the beams for the roof. They were far too long to be able to bring them up in the jeep so we had to carry every back breaking one up to the house from the plateia ourselves. Papa Kostas and I had negotiated a price for the job based on a daily rate, rather than price per square metre where, in Greece, you have one price for stonework, another for brickwork, another for floor laying and yet a different one for roofing. The complexities of this method make it almost impossible to check the calculations finally submitted, against original estimates, and I wanted a clear idea of what it was going to cost. Everything was ready for him to start but, when I asked him when that would be, he became disconcertingly vague. "In a few days," was the best I could get out of him.

After ten days he turned up, eager and willing. A couple of days later he'd laid the foundations and the floor, and then promptly disappeared for a week to build a stone lychgate, a commission he'd got on the back of building ours. After that he put up a fence at the other end of the village before eventually returning, building the inside walls, and vanishing again. This mercurial behaviour was beginning to test my usual good humour. I decided to go down to his house and find out what was going on. Why was he giving us the miss? We had, after all, discussed this project back in December when he had no work scheduled and now, with other work coming in, we were being dropped to the end of the queue.

From tentative questioning it transpired that he didn't want to be paid by the day, but by the square metre. Reluctantly I gave in and agreed to this but on condition the building would be finished quickly. Smiling over his chipero Papa Kostas said he would get David to help him and they would get it done in no time. He would start on Wednesday. Effie and I had arranged to go to Corfu for a week to catch up with friends and take a short break. We were leaving on the Wednesday, and set off with nervous doubts about the wisdom of going at all only to find on our return that nothing had been done.

When we did get back however, we were met by the sight of an almost completed building. Only half the roof stones remained to be laid, and an interior dividing wall put up. We were delighted, and a beaming Papa Kostas embraced us.

"Wonderful! Good work Kostas!" I said, hugging him, and all my previous fears were washed away with a friendly glass of wine.

The next day he started work on re-roofing a massive old mansion in the centre of the village and he didn't do any work for us during the next month. His beaming smile whenever I ran into him was becoming increasingly irritating. I came to a decision. In Ioannina I loaded Suzi with bricks, piled them outside the new building and with string and balance started building the dividing wall myself. Two more loads of bricks and the wall was completed. A first time effort that I was both proud of and felt better for inasmuch as I was confident now that I could, if necessary, finish the building myself. Just as I was about to embark on continuing with the roof, Papa Kostas turned up and finished it himself, leaving the internal rendering still to be done. At this point another disappearing act nearly drove me into the hands of little men in white coats, but I was saved by his relatively prompt return after a few days. He finished the rendering in a continual run and as the last bit of wall was covered I could feel my body returning to its normal, relaxed self. Papa Kostas had at last finished the apotheeki!

Standing back to admire his work, he said, "Now! I know a man who can make the windows for you. Not expensive - and quickly, too."

"Quickly?" I repeated, trying to remember what the word meant and wondering where he had got it from. The thought of Papa Kostas with his organisational skills acting as an intermediary with a third party to put the windows in filled me with horror. I explained that Apostolis already had a man making them which, although not strictly true, was near enough the mark to avoid any further delays.

During the following weeks we painted, put up shelves and moved in all the tools from the old workshop. We unpacked boxes of forgotten treasures, and not having room in our little house for any more, packed them up again and put them back into store. At last the hotel building was cleared, ready for the day Mitsos and his bobcat would begin their assault. For the moment I had had enough of builders and building - I needed a break. Or so I thought, until Effie had an inspiration. She'd found the perfect spot for a greenhouse, facing south, sun all day long, sheltered from the east...!

We were still getting a trickle of friends arriving to seek us out, and with the workshop empty, de-cobwebbed, swept clean of sawdust, with curtains and a folding bed a sort of guest room was available for the hardy; those preferring more salubrious accommodation we continued to book into the 'Pension Artemis' in Kipi. The villagers had grown accustomed to our flow of visitors and generally liked the idea of foreigners taking the trouble to come to their village to look at and admire it. One of Petros' brothers, a retired history teacher, would latch himself onto them and whisk them off on a guided tour, to the Lazarides Museum, the square, the well arches, explaining the history of Koukouli in microscopic detail. Undeterred by the fact that most of them couldn't understand a word of what he said, his enthusiasm and love of subject transcended language. On their return to our house, glassy eyed and battle weary with half understood knowledge, Effie would fill them in with the more salient points.

Time had marched on and we suddenly realised that we were nearing the completion of our first twelve months in Koukouli. The signs of summer ending and autumn approaching we had seen before. The first summer people were starting to leave and David the Albanian was preparing to go back to his wife and child. With earnings of 3,000 drachmas a day, and little to spend it on, he had, deservedly, amassed a considerable fortune by Albanian standards. For security, Papa Kostas had acted as his banker, a tin hut hardly being thought a safe place to stash money, and he was far from happy with the idea of David trudging back on foot across the mountains with such a sum. Particularly with other Albanians, penniless from their own country, walking in the opposite direction. Also David, whose good humoured grin and gangling personality had made him popular in the village, found he had been given an overwhelming collection of cast-offs. Blankets, pillows, tools, clothes, children's toys, all sorts of things which would be of useful value back home. It would be impossible for him to struggle back with all these new possessions. So, after some considerable trouble, they managed to speak to David's brother over the telephone and arranged for him to be at the border early morning, ready to accompany David on the onward bus journey home. At crack of dawn, Papa Kostas drove him, his gear and his hard earned wealth to the rendezvous, and saw them safely reunited.

Despite the glorious weather, with David gone and others leaving, summer felt over. The talk of logs had started up again and Papa Kostas was adamant that this year we should not have to buy expensive logs. Both Michalis and Vasilia had offered to let us have trees from parcels of land they owned behind the village, but we would need to find Dimitris, a rakish young fellow from Kapesovo whom we knew, to come down with his chain saw and truck, to cut and cart the wood. One evening we were summonsed to go down to Papa Kostas' to try and organise this business with Dimitris over the telephone.

When we arrived, a little after nine o'clock, we found Papa Kostas and Kiki had gone off to sweep the church in readiness for a christening next day. The family had just finished their supper and the kitchen looked as if a bomb had hit it. Elevtheria was kneeling on the floor bottle-feeding an early lamb. On her instruction we helped ourselves to chipero and cleared a place to sit. Then the phone rang. Effie suddenly found a lamb and feeding bottle dumped on her lap as Elevtheria went for the receiver. It was Marigoula, from the other end of the village. With unusual tension in her voice she jabbered that three people, arriving by car, had seen the light in her kitchen and knocked at the door, asking directions to the church and Papa Kostas' house. One of the three she recognised as a high ranking Bishop from Ioannina!

We were all galvanised into action. Georgos was dispatched to take the lamb back to the shed, then find Papa Kostas and warn him. Effie grabbed some damp washing hanging round the wood-burner and threw it in a cupboard under the stairs. The table was cleared and wiped clean, washing up disposed of or hidden. I whisked round with the vacuum cleaner; children's books, shoes, satchels and toys were dumped in the adjoining room; cushions were straightened, curtains pulled into shape, things about the room tidied and all done in rapid motion like some silent movie. Finally Elevtheria brushed her hair and we all sat down, po-faced, in seemingly utter composure, awaiting the arrival of the Bishop.

He, accompanied by his driver and the driver's wife, had gone to the church and found Papa Kostas. When they all entered the kitchen, the contrast between the Papas and the Bishop, both working as it were for the same firm, was comical. Kostas was in his threadbare, working jeans and wool vest with a crumpled denim jacket slung across his shoulders. The habitual cocktail stick was protruding from plaster encrusted hair; his bare feet were shod in over-sized rubber flip-flops. The Bishop, in his early thirties, lived a monastic life as an academic and scholar on the island in Lake Pamvotis. He was tall, somewhat regal in bearing, with neatly polished and manicured nails. His simple blue cassock was of the finest cloth and intricately embroidered in discreetly darker blue around the edges. The collar of his silk shirt was pristine. Gold rimmed glasses sat upon a slightly hooked nose, hiding a pair of wonderfully calm yet humorous eyes. His wavy black hair was receding and his skin as smooth as waxed vellum without a line upon it. This man was, without doubt, something of a dandy.

After introductions we all sat around the table whilst Kiki and an extremely nervous Elevtheria prepared mezedes, and Papa Kostas, unabashed by the honour of this visit, offered his wine. Conversation at first was staccato but the proof of Kostas' wine soon produced a more relaxed, informal atmosphere, greatly helped by the charm and easy manner of the Bishop. The topics of conversation became more varied and animated and we found ourselves being courteously drawn in wherever possible. It was close on midnight when the Bishop announced that unfortunately he was expected in another village before returning to Ioannina and he would have to take his leave. He extended an open invitation to all of us to visit him at the monastery on the island.

Our initial apprehension over his unexpected visit had proved to be unfounded. But still I couldn't help wondering what a Bishop of his standing was doing visiting a village priest, unannounced, late at night? Was the girl, whose eyes all evening rarely strayed from his face, really anything to do with the driver? And why were they going on to another village at that late hour? Who knows.

A new school year had begun, with the usual worries for the children at the prospect of a new teacher, new syllabus and a different class. The nearest school for Papa Kostas' four was in Karies, the largish modern township half an hour's drive down the mountains towards Ioannina. Every morning, rain or shine, either Elevtheria or Papa Kostas had to set off at half past seven to get them to school for eight. If they were late they suffered quite severe penalties, so mornings in their household between seven and half past were fraught.

One day, after the first week of term, our phone rang at a quarter to eight. It was an agitated Kiki. Could I please take them to school - they were without a car! Struggling into clothes and mercifully finding my keys first go, I hurried down to their house. Four woebegone faces met me at the corner and they piled themselves into the jeep. At a bend on the track down to the main road, we passed an open truck with its offside wing in a close embrace with the offside wing of the family's Lada! It was the most unfortunate coincidence that plumbers, coming to do some work for Kleoniki, should have been driving up the track never expecting to meet downcoming traffic, just at the same time as Papa Kostas was setting off on the school run, never expecting to meet upcoming traffic. How many times over the years can he have met anyone coming up to the village at that early hour? Practically never, so doubtless he was driving in his own irrepressible style. Fortunately the accident wasn't serious; no-one was hurt and the children were close enough to home to scamper quickly back. But, Kostas' Toyota pickup was in the garage having a new tailgate fitted. They were stuck! I was the only other person in the village with a car.

And so there I was, driving down to Karies, being urged by all four to go "Faster! FASTER!!" The responsibility of having the Papas' entire progeny on board and in my care far outweighed my sympathy for them being late, and it was nearly half past eight when we swung into the school yard. They tumbled out of the car and pelted into the building without a backward glance, vague "Thank yous" fading in their slipstream.

The problem with the Greek school system is that having started at eight, they are out by one thirty. I got home just after nine, shaved and breakfasted and then had to be off again at one o'clock to pick them up. By a quarter past two we were all back in Koukouli, the children in time for lunch followed by homework. Two journeys down and back, taking an hour each. And this is Papa Kostas and Elevtheria's routine, five days a week during term time. Combined with clerical duties, building work, keeping up with their allotments, goats and chicken, housekeeping, washing, cooking and attending to the everyday needs of the children it was no wonder they laboured from dawn to dusk!

Kostas was to collect the car on the Friday afternoon, so for the rest of the week Uncle Roy and Suzi were on school duty. The following day I found Elevtheria in going-out clothes standing on the corner with the children. She wanted to come with us to Karies from where she would catch a bus to Ioannina. Somehow all four kids managed to squeeze into the back and Elevtheria took the passenger seat. From outside the car seemed to have a sea of faces at every window. I'd planned to go on to Ioannina myself that day - pay the electricity bill, go to the post office, buy a newspaper - so Elevtheria and I went on together. Having arranged a meeting point we returned to Karies and the disgruntled children once more had to jig-saw themselves into the back.

Friday was my last day. There on the corner, with the children grinning all over their faces, was Elevtheria, AND Papa Kostas in cassock and hat. They all wanted to come! I watched, open mouthed, as they jammed themselves into Suzi, Papa Kostas in the passenger seat with Elevtheria on his knee, her head touching the roof. As I started up I jokingly asked them where their dog, Bummer, was.

"On the roof!" laughed Papa Kostas, gesturing dangerously out of the open window.

So we bundled along, like The Buggins Family. At Karies, Papa Kostas and Elevtheria went on by bus to collect the car. All that was left for me to do was pick up the children at the usual time and bring them home. Then, for Suzi and me, the school run was over.

Koukouli was once more in winter mode, seemingly deserted. Two late tourists turned up outside our gate, wrapped in heavy parkas, admiring Papa Kostas' stonework. They looked blue with cold, and the kafeneon we knew was closed, so we invited them in for coffee. They hadn't visited Zagoria before but friends of theirs had, and had told them to make a point of visiting Koukouli. Driving through to Tsepelovo they had picked up the roadsign for the village and approached not from our end, the church end, but the other end where the buses have their turning area. From this approach you see nothing to suggest the presence of a village at all, except for a breeze block bus shelter with a steel barred door. However, knowing their friends must have found something that attracted them they persevered and found their way into the village.

It had been mid-afternoon and they'd strolled along the lower street, past the church and plateia and taken the top lane back to the car. In the course of half an hour they had not seen a living soul. It was, they said, like being on the Marie Celeste. They had noted some fine, impressive mansions but also equally impressive ruins, crumbling walls, gates lolling on one hinge and windows about to fall in once gravity could no longer support them. They had returned today mid-morning in the hope they might, at that time of the day, find people about. Sitting on the stone wall round the plane tree was Petros' son and a friend hanging around waiting to go up to university, idling the time playing cards. Seeing signs of life at last, they had gone up to them and eagerly asked the question that had been worrying them.

"Isn't there anybody in this village doing anything to restore some of these beautiful old buildings?"

In unison there came the reply:

"Only the Papas and the Englishman."

ALSO FROM YIANNIS BOOKS

In 1966, John Waller and his Danish wife visit the island. In the days before charter flights and package tours, Corfu is 'heaven on earth'. In 1971 they buy a plot of land above undiscovered Agios Gordis on the west coast and build a modest summer house. They discover the sometimes high financial and emotional cost of possessing 'Greek Walls'.

Corfu Sunset
Avrio Never Comes

John Waller

Illustrated by John Chipperfield

Avrio never comes, the sequel to ***Greek Walls*** is a comedy in three parts:

● regaining control from Spiros Grammenos, the neighbour;
● a frenetic summer building a road up the mountain and a pool, veranda and new roof for the villa; and
● a party to celebrate a great Greek victory.

Roy Hounsell was born in Woldingham, Surrey in 1942 and educated at Millfield College, Somerset. In 1980, as Marketing and Advertising Manager of a Household and Furnishing Department, he was made redundant.

'The Papas and the Englishman – from Corfu to Zagoria' is his first book.